WORK, PLAY, AND WORSHIP

IN A LEISURE-ORIENTED SOCIETY

GORDON DAHL

AUGSBURG PUBLISHING HOUSE
MINNEAPOLIS, MINNESOTA

WORK, PLAY, AND WORSHIP

Copyright © 1972 Augsburg Publishing House

Library of Congress Catalog Card No. 72-78566

International Standard Book No. 0-8066-1233-9

Scripture quotations unless otherwise noted are from the Revised Standard Version of the Bible, copyright 1946 and 1952 by the Division of Christian Education of the National Council of Churches, and are used by permission.

Manufactured in the United States of America

Contents

48222

Preface

This is a book about leisure.

A book about leisure should be written leisurely. This one was. Most of its content has emerged from periods of reflection and discussions with friends over the past several years. Portions of it have been presented to groups of students, clergymen, parents, and teachers in assorted seminars and workshops. Bits of it have found their way into articles and sermons. These efforts have been purposive and disciplined, and hopefully they reflect a serious and significant endeavor, but they have been leisurely, nevertheless.

A book about leisure should not be expected to be a finished product. This one is not. While these may not be the first ideas I have had concerning these matters, I certainly hope they are not my last! I have decided to share them in this form, not because they are finished, but in hopes of stimulating a wider discussion of work, play, and worship in an age of leisure. Hopefully, these ideas will generate some reactions — even some arguments — among Christians who are trying to analyze and arrange their priorities in these times of great fascination and great frustration.

A book about leisure should offer possibilities for both liberation and renewal. This one has so done for its author and, hopefully, it will do that for some others — especially some of those who are experiencing conflict between their sense of Christian discipleship and their participation in a leisure-oriented society.

Finally, a book about leisure should be an expression of gratitude for the joys and meanings which life has afforded. This one is most certainly that! To here identify everyone and everything for whom or which I feel gratitude would, of course, be neither appropriate nor relevant. But there is one special group — my associates in Leisure Studies, Incorporated — that deserves special mention, for without their encouragement and assistance this book would not have been written.

GORDON J. DAHL

P.S. By the way, a book about leisure should be read *leisurely*.

1

Work, Play, and Worship

Today, as in other eras, the daily lives of Christians revolve around their work, their play, and their worship.

By work, of course, we could mean all those things which we must do to assure our survival, to promote our personal well-being, and to fulfill our responsibilities to society. For most of us, however, our work consists primarily of those more or less obligatory activities which are related to our occupation or profession. When we speak of work today, therefore, we are usually talking about our job — or our lack of a job.

By play, we usually mean those things which we do — not because we have to but because we want to — for our own enjoyment or pleasure and to experience special delights in our relationship with others. In a sense, we can play almost anytime — even when we are working — but most of us think of play as being

7

something separated from our work. In fact, many people consider play to be the opposite of work.

And by worship, we usually mean that set of attitudes and activities by which we affirm our relationship to God and attune our lives to his purposes. Like work and play, worship can be defined very broadly — and can be experienced in many ways — but most of us regard worship as that which is taking place when we consciously invoke the spirit of God in some matter of private concern or in some corporate assembly.

There are many more complex and sophisticated definitions of work, play and worship, but these will be adequate for the purposes of this book. Under these three broad and commonplace categories, we will discuss the character of Christian life in contemporary American society — a society which is becoming increasingly dominated by the pursuit of leisure and its challenges. (A definition of leisure, as well as some descriptions of a leisure oriented society, will be presented in the chapters which follow.)[1]

For most Christians, work, play and worship are somewhat related. Clear-cut distinctions, at least, often cannot and, indeed, should not be made. Ideally, no distinctions should exist and many persons experience their greatest joy when they engage in some activity which combines all three — work, play and worship. In reality, however, distinctions do exist and most people today experience more of the separation than the integration of these components. That is, most contemporary Americans, including those who consider themselves and struggle to be Christians, experience life as fragments of work, fragments of play, and fragments of worship. There are all too few experiences of their harmony and wholeness. As a result, their work, their play and their worship are often haunted by a disturbing sense of meaninglessness. And in spite of the unprecedented opportunities which modern Americans have to work, to play and to worship in freedom and fellowship, their lives are often engulfed by a pervasive loneliness that prevents them from enjoying and sharing their abundance.

Both Scripture and Christian tradition are loaded with pious counsel concerning work, play and worship, but they offer no adequate formula for their integration into a contemporary Christian life-style. This book will not offer any formula either, but it will attempt to show that some fresh evaluations of these components are both necessary and desirable. In fact, the primary purpose of this book is to show that a new consciousness of the meanings and relationships of these three elements of our daily lives — work, play and worship — can offer the key to both human survival and Christian renewal in a time of fantastic social and technological change.

Although their contents will consist largely of interpretations of present trends, the chapters which follow are intended to provide some basic orientation to the future. This orientation assumes, however, that contemporary Christians will find both their greatest clarity about their own identity and destiny and their most relevant role in their larger society in a radical reconsideration of their own biblical and theological heritage amidst a frank and realistic assessment of their current economic and social systems.

To avoid misunderstandings, however, let it be clear that the purpose of this book is neither to revise religious traditions nor reform social systems — although the need for revisions and reforms will be often exposed. Our real aim in these brief chapters is to help Christians — especially young, active, ambitious and talented adult Americans — renew their understanding of themselves and their involvement in the life of this strange and fascinating world as they work, play and worship.

2

Leisure? Ha!
I'm Busier than Ever

The common complaint of contemporary Americans, young and old, rich and poor, is that they are too busy. We frequently find ourselves apologizing and lamenting that we are too busy ourselves — and we are often hurt by the discovery that others are too busy for us. Yet, for all our busy-ness, we never seem to experience anything that approaches fulfillment or transcendence. And those who would seem to have the greatest opportunities for leisure are often among those who find it to be most elusive.

Perhaps the reason why so many modern men and women are having difficulty integrating their lives, and thereby finding meaning and satisfying relationships, is because they are confused about the roles which their work, their play and their worship are playing in their lives. Most Americans believe and practice these three things but few have adequately or creatively integrated them into their life style.

To put it sharply, most middle-class Americans tend to worship their work, to work at their play, and to play at their worship. As a result, their meanings and values are distorted, their relationships disintegrate faster than they can keep them in repair, and their life styles resemble a cast of characters in search of a plot.

Among other things, this confusion about work, play and worship has generated false and superficial notions about leisure. Among those imbued with middle-class mores, leisure is regarded with either a suspicious and judgmental attitude or with a prurient interest — depending upon how strong those mores stand in the face of tempting alternatives. In any case, the leisure revolution is compelling a reconsideration of the roles of work, play and worship in both our personal life styles and our social systems. Hopefully, the result will be to emancipate our concepts of leisure from their negative free-time and non-work connotations in order to help us achieve fuller experiences of freedom and thus find the richer dimensions of fulfillment and transcendence.

The Problem: We worship our work.

If a stranger approaches and asks "Who are you?" how do you reply? Or, how do you generally introduce yourself to a new group? The odds are that after offering your name, and perhaps the name of your city or town, you will identify yourself in terms of your work, i.e., your job or occupation. So will nearly everyone else you encounter. In our society, work is probably the most important determinant of personal identity. To participate in our society, therefore, means that you will define yourself, and allow others to define you, on the basis of the work you do.

But is it only your identity which is defined by work? Where do you live? When do you sleep or play? How do you dress and groom yourself? What people do you associate with? What determines your day-to-day, month-to-month routine? What prevents you from changing this routine? On what do you depend for food and shelter?

The answer that most of us will give to these questions will be, directly or indirectly, our work. In other words, work not only defines our identity in society; it also shapes most of the directions and dynamics of our lives. In fact, participation in our social systems demands that we arrange our lives around our work.

It is not surprising, therefore, that work is often assigned universal and unqualified value. It becomes the basis for measuring human worth. It is offered as a solution to personal and social problems. It is considered the foundation of our social and economic systems. Without a nearly universal commitment to the value of work, our society would collapse!

Think about that for a moment. How are men ranked and rewarded in a democratic society? It is usually on the basis of their accomplishment at work. What is our favorite panacea for the distress of the poor, the minorities, and the rebellious young in our society? "Make them work!" And what do we consider the primary objective of our political economy? A job for everyone — even if it has to be created or supported by governmental action. Work, in short, is the god of our system!

Work is both good and necessary. In fact, work is both *very* good and *very* necessary. But its goodness is not intrinsic and its necessity is not ultimate — at least not from any Christian point of view. Work is important and it makes sense to pursue it with diligence, honesty and pride. But work is not to be worshipped and glorified. Work is not the basis for human dignity or worth. Work saves no man from sin, death or the power of the devil, in spite of what all the pious and secular moralists of history have tried to make us believe.

Work should indeed be regarded as both good and necessary, but when it is allowed to function as the chief determinant of human identity as well as the index of human worth, it dehumanizes men and their relationships. When it locks men and women into value systems and life styles in order to support particular socio-economic systems, especially when those systems ascribe unto themselves some sort of metaphysical authority or origin, work becomes a demonic force. When work becomes the all-consuming interest of a man, even if his work is good and necessary, it is idolatry.

Contemporary American Christians have inherited both a system of economic and social institutions and a system of moral and religious values that almost compel us to practice idolatry in relation to work or drop out of these inherited systems. We are caught up in a spreading scheme of manipulative materialism that from any reference point outside our own time and place would be recognized as sin — not only because it promotes individual comfort and security above all other ends but also because it is destroying our natural, our human, and our cultural environments.

Work is good and necessary, but our worship of work allows us to work at things which are neither good nor necessary. The men whose work it is to make napalm and fragmentation bombs are probably very diligent and honest. They certainly do not consider themselves murderers, even though death and destruction are the intended consequences of their work. Their idolatry with respect to work and their loyalty to the systems which perpetuate (and are perpetuated by) that idolatry blind them to the larger moral implications of their work. Work can be as destructive as it can be creative. Indeed, some work is evil!

Not everyone who worships work, of course, makes instruments of death, but the day will come when many of us, or at least many of our heirs, will say, "It would have been better to have never worked." Remember, the very first of the Ten Commandments was the prohibition of idolatry. We have other idols today, also, but the greatest idol for most contemporary Americans, including most Christians, is that which is called "My work."

The Problem: We work at our play.

The idolatry we commit with respect to work also perverts our understanding of play. Lest it interfere with our work, our play is usually separated from it by both time and space. Play is appropriate only after hours (after work hours), weekends (after the work week ends), and holidays or vacations (days we are legitimately exempted from work). Furthermore, most play is confined to certain places, i.e., preserves or compounds such as parks, playgrounds, gymnasiums, resorts, or clubs, where the character of the play can be defined and circumscribed. Many of these places even come equipped with professionals who are there to tell us how (or how not) to play. In other words, play in modern American society is almost as much of a conditioned and controlled activity as work, in spite of the fact that most Americans think of play primarily as freedom from work.

To make matters worse, many of us find our work continually encroaching upon even those areas which are reserved for play. Play time is usually preempted whenever work demands. The result is often a confusing mixture of business and pleasure that only further stifles human freedom and takes joy out of life. As Walter Kerr put it a few years ago:

> We are all of us compelled to read for profit, party for contacts, lunch for contracts, bowl for unity, drive for mileage, gamble for charity, go out for the evening for the greater glory of the municipality, and stay home for the weekend to rebuild the house.[1]

In other words, even those times and places which are set aside for play become co-opted for interests related to work, thus perverting the pleasure they are intended to provide by making them serve alien interests.

Play is also perverted by the tendency of so many Americans to carry into it the same aggressive, competitive, and manipulative traits that are cultivated in them by their work. Many use play as an outlet for tensions that are built up, but not satisfactorily released, by their work experience. A man may not dare demonstrate his superior knowledge and skill over another who outranks him on the job, for example, but he will try to establish his rightful superiority by beating him in golf or by throwing a bigger party. A female employee who may not be able to achieve better salary and working conditions on the basis of her performance at work will sometimes find it possible to gain these things from her male employer by playing with him after work.

The most serious casualties of the perversion of play, however, are to be found among those who work at jobs which are so sedentary and unchallenging and whose faculties for play are so undeveloped that they crave violence for the discharge of their energies and the release of their tensions. Everyone needs outlets for physical energy and opportunities for mental exercise. Outdoor recreation, participatory sports and many arts and crafts offer great opportunities for this kind of play with very little or no violence to one another or to our environment. Unfortunately, however, some people prefer to seek their release through vicious use of the environment or through vicarious play — by merely watching the physical and mental activity of others on a football field or theater stage or television screen — which often means that they need a display of brutality or devastation to become actually involved in the action and passion.

Life's greatest tragedy for many Americans today, however, is that they simply do not know how to play. Without some kind of noisy machine to ride around in or on, they are utterly helpless as far as play is concerned. If a Camus or Kafka were to come to the United States today in search of a prototype to illustrate the hopelessness of modern man's situation, he would undoubtedly scan that long line of automobiles heading away from any metropolis on Friday evenings, pulling trailers with either a boat, or a camper, or a pair of motor-bikes or snowmobiles, or combinations of these "play" things. Frantically squeezing the steering wheel of almost any one of these autos would be a middle-class American, a worker of either the blue or white collar species, intermittently cursing the traffic, listening for the weather report and muttering to his harried wife and howling kids, "By golly, this weekend we're going to relax!" That same man will be in that same line of cars heading back to the city Sunday night. The only difference is that he will then be too exhausted to complain about the traffic. He may even be looking forward to going back to work the next day in order to rest.

The Problem: We play at our worship.

The one place left for play in the lives of many Americans is, alas, their worship. What most Americans do in the name of worship has no significant relationship to anything they consider important in the real world. In fact, most worship occasions are used to transport us to some other world on flights of aesthetic and historical fantasy. In many traditional worship services, the only concern with the here and now is during the announcements and when the offering is received. The liturgy, the hymns, and often the sermon belong to another age. The minister, the choir, and many members of the congregation put on special costumes and everybody pretends to be praising God and confessing their sins, and loving one another whether anyone really means it or not. In other words, our worship is some sort of game we play each week (that is, if we do not have work to do). Our worship is play. Pedagogical and perhaps therapeutic play, to be sure, but play, nevertheless. (Even when the liturgical buffs make us work hard at it.)

The fact that our worship is play does not negate its significance or value. In fact, since play is the highest form of human behavior, it is altogether appropriate that when people gather to celebrate their relationship to God and to each other they should play.

What we generally call worship, however, and what the Scriptures call for as worship are quite different. In the Scriptures, worship is depicted as a total life response to God and his plan for our salvation. St. Paul says to the Romans:

> I appeal to you, therefore, brethren, by the mercies
> of God, to present your bodies as a living sacrifice,
> holy and acceptable to God, which is your spiritual
> worship.[2]

In other words, worship is the full commitment of
one's life to God. But we have made our work the
primary dimension of our lives, so it is little wonder
that we experience worship as little more than an
occasional pious exercise. Worship should encompass
all our work and all our play, but what we practice
in the church relates to only small fragments of our
work and play. In fact, our idolatry about work and
our ignorance about play makes it difficult, almost
embarrassing, to celebrate our worship. So we go
through the motions, pretending to be involved, but
most of the time we are only participating in a feeble
form of play.

That brings us around the circle. We worship our
work. We work at our play. And we play at our worship. The ingredients for a faithful and joyful Christian life are all there, but we have the formula confused.

The Opportunity: The Work-God is Dead.

As long as people are working and are finding their
work meaningful and rewarding, they scarcely notice
what they are missing as far as play and worship are
concerned. When they are separated from their work,
however, or when their work loses its challenge, a
profound disillusionment sets in. Having allowed their

jobs to determine their personal identity and their social relationships, they have nothing left when their job is finished or taken away. To those who worship work, unemployment or retirement represent threats to more than just their economic welfare. To many, they signal the end of life.

To increasing numbers of Americans, however, and especially to American youth, the work-god is dead. That in essence, is the meaning of the so-called "leisure revolution." The dynamics of that revolution will be discussed in the next chapter, but the point is that future generations of Americans will not have the same reverence for work that their forefathers have had. Work will still be good and necessary, but it will not provide as fully either the personal satisfaction or the social salvation as it once did. Already, more and more people are looking elsewhere for the meaning and purpose of their lives.

Up to this point, most of our leaders (including leaders of churches) have greeted this trend simply in terms of the question: What will take the place of work? It is not surprising, therefore, that their responses to the leisure revolution have usually been superficial. Most of the concern about leisure has resulted only in new forms of distraction designed to take people's minds off the fact that if they are working less they are worth less in our society. (And if they are not working at all, they are a burden.)

Many worshippers of work, of course, will never admit that their god is dead or that their ethic is no longer viable. Fearing that the leisure revolution will bring moral anarchy and social chaos, some church-men are already praying for a resurrection, i.e., a return to the virtues of hard work. Since American religion has faithfully supported the work system and since religious institutions have often led the way in creating places for society to dump its nonworking members, i.e., its aged, its handicapped, its young, it is altogether possible that some churches will be the last strongholds for the idolatry of work.

But those who continue to worship at the altars of work, and who refuse to recognize the values of play and the full meaning of worship, will be swept away by the leisure revolution. As the distinguished historian, Arnold Toynbee has written, our technology is not merely allowing us more leisure; it is imposing more leisure upon us than was ever known by our prede-cessors. Toynbee correctly notes that modern man's work has provided him with acceptable alternatives to facing God as well as a respectable anesthetic with which to cope with the ironies and ambiguities of human life. But no more.

> Work is going to become as rare and costly an anesthetic as the most strictly prohibited drug. The majority of us will have to live without the anes-thetic of factory or office work. The conveyor-belt that enabled us, in the archaic phase of industry, to evade confrontation with God will now eject us into God's presence.[3]

What is needed is not a resusitation of the dead idol, nor merely a replacement, but a radical reconsideration of the meaning and purpose of human life — a reconsideration which includes some clearer understanding of all three of the elements we have discussed — work, play, and worship — and some new arrangement in their priorities and relationships.

The leisure revolution offers the opportunity for this reconsideration — in fact, it compels it whether we like it or not. Most Americans, however, and especially most middle-class Christians, will have to revise their understanding of leisure before we can take advantage of that opportunity. The next few chapters will discuss the dynamics of the leisure revolution and offer some new concepts with which to cope with it.

3

What Do You Mean
—A Leisure Revolution?

Before proceeding any farther into the conceptual and spiritual aspects of leisure, it is important that we get some perspective on the contemporary cultural context in which our attempts to experience and understand leisure are taking place. Those who think of leisure primarily in terms of free time or non-work have often limited their attention to phenomena related to recreation and retirement. They have thus seen only fragments of the larger economic and social trends which collectively comprise a "leisure revolution." Indeed, there are few Americans who have yet begun to consider the full range of factors and forces which are contributing to this revolution.

The purpose of this chapter, therefore, is to offer a profile of the leisure revolution by briefly describing each of ten contributing trends. These trends vary in scope and significance, but they represent the changes in our personal and social patterns which are facilitating the emergence of a leisure-oriented society. Each of these trends is far more complex than its treatment in this chapter will suggest and several of them have already been the focus of special studies and writings. More studies and evaluations are needed, but our primary objective here is to simply summarize these various developments to show the magnitude of the so-called "leisure revolution."

The Major Trends Toward a Leisure-Oriented Society

1. Shorter work days and work weeks.

In 1850, the average American worker spent 70 hours per week at his job. By 1900, the average work week had been reduced to 60 hours and by 1920 to 50 hours. By 1935, the 40-hour week became a standard and by 1965 many union contracts called for a 35-hour week. There are indications that the trend toward shorter work weeks is leveling off, but 30- and even 25-hour contracts are no longer uncommon.[1]

It is not only the size, but also the shape, of the work week which is changing. Experiments with a four day week in many industries have proven successful and there is every indication that it will become a standard in some of them whether or not the total hours per week changes.

Riva Poor, who edited a best-selling book on the four day work week in 1970, reported that within less than eight months of her book's publication she became aware of almost 400 American firms, and more than 100 companies in Australia, Canada, France, and Great Britain, that have adapted the four day week on at least a trial basis.[2] In July, 1971, the Village of Minnetonka, a suburb of Minneapolis, Minnesota, laid claim to being the first governmental agency to place its employees on a four day work week.[3]

In September, 1971, the California legislature passed enabling legislation to permit any state agency that so desires to adopt a four day week for its employees. The October, 1971, issue of *Playboy* magazine cites a prediction by a labor-management consultant that 80% of American industry will be operating on a four day week within five years. *Playboy* also reports that computer personnel at two large insurance companies are experimenting with a work week of *three* days of 12 hours each.[4]

2. *Longer vacations and holidays.*

By ancient standards, the number of holidays observed by most Americans is comparatively few. Fourth century Romans, for example, observed as many as 175 special days and throughout the Middle Ages most of the Christiandom celebrated between 100 and 125 "holy days" each year. The combined effects of the Protestant Reformation and the Industrial Revolution drastically reduced the frequency of holidays, however, especially in those countries where Protestantism and industrialism became the major forces in shaping social patterns.

Since the beginning of the twentieth century, Americans have been steadily increasing their days of exemption from work by increasing both the number of holidays and the length of vacation periods. In 1971, the holiday schedule was revised so as to make at least five holidays each year into three day weekends. Furthermore, 95 per cent of all American workers now have at least two weeks of vacation per year and nearly 50 per cent have three weeks or more. Extended vacation time has become a major fringe benefit in collective bargaining arrangements and is a basic form of reward for seniority and special service.

As a result of the combination of shorter work weeks and longer vacations, the average American worker of today has nearly 1,200 more hours per year of non-working time than did his grandfather living before the turn of the century.[5]

3. Extended periods of education and retirement.

The periods of time an average American spends in school before entering the work force and after his retirement have been increasing steadily. Between 1960 and 1970, for example, the proportion of high school graduates rose from 41 to 55 percent of the adult population and the proportion of college graduates moved from 8 to 11 per cent.

Young adults and persons who are retired are generally considered to have more leisure and leisure interests. Both groups have been growing steadily, both in actual numbers and in their proportion of the total population. In 1960, for example, there were about 11 million persons in the 20-24 year old age group and they comprised 6.1 per cent of the population. By 1970, their numbers had increased to 17.2 million and their proportion to 8.4 per cent. By 1980 they will number 20.9 million and represent 9 per cent of all Americans.

During these same decades, the numbers of persons 62 years and older have increased from 20.7 million in 1960, to 24.7 in 1970 and to a projected 29.2 million in 1980. This group comprised 11.5 per cent of the population in 1960, 12 per cent in 1970, and will be 12.6 per cent in 1980.[6]

Leisure opportunities for older people are being expanded by both increases in life expectancy and the lowering of the retirement age. Advances in health care and programs of economic security are also enhancing the quality as well as the quantity of these later years, even though much more needs to be done to assure those who are no longer working a full share of the security and well being they deserve as members of American society.

4. Steadily rising personal income.

In spite of the fact that millions are still living in poverty, most American families have experienced substantial increases in income during the past decades and will be enjoying even greater affluence in the decades ahead. Per capita income after taxes, for example, rose 37 per cent between 1960 and 1970 even with allowances for inflation. The proportion of families receiving an annual income of $10,000 or more grew from 25 to 46 per cent.[7]

The economic recession of 1970-71 caused severe problems of inflation and unemployment, but, significantly, it did not halt the steady rise in personal incomes of those Americans who comprise the work force.

Based upon economic trends since 1950, Hudson Institute economists have predicted that by the year 2000 at least one-fourth of the families in America will have incomes equivalent to $25,000 as measured in 1965 dollars. One-twelfth of these families will have incomes over $50,000.[8]

A 1967 University of Michigan survey of consumer finances showed that spending for leisure activities and products increases rapidly as personal income rises. Increased income not only induces more families to spend money on leisure, but it also increases the size of their investment. This survey found that the most active consumers of leisure products and services were families with annual incomes between $10,000 and $15,000.[9]

5. Development of leisure industries.

Paralleling the rise in personal incomes has been the development of leisure industries. In fact, leisure has now become one of the major growth areas in the American economy with total annual sales of leisure products and services estimated at figures up to 150 billion dollars, depending upon what is counted as leisure.

A glance at some particular industries will illustrate the trend: More than two million American families now own second homes and another million second homes will be built in the seventies. Nearly nine million pleasure boats are used on U.S. waterways and annual retail expenditures for boating have increased from 2.5 billion to 3.4 billion during the past decade. The National Sporting Goods Association reported that $86,500,000 worth of tents and $59,200,000 worth of sleeping bags were sold in 1970, figures that were nearly double those of 1960.[10]

Attendance at sports events increased by 60 per cent during the sixties, while multiplying numbers of golfers, fishermen, bowlers, skiers, tennis players, and archers created demands for more and more equipment and facilities. Providing golfing equipment alone requires an industry grossing $250 million a year. Another quarter-billion dollars is spent on fishing tackle.[11]

Recreational vehicles, especially snowmobiles and the various kinds of campers, have been the basis for another several billions of dollars in industrial growth. Almost unheard of in 1960, the snowmobile industry in the United States and Canada reached an annual production of more than half a million machines in the 1970-71 season. The Recreational Vehicle Institute estimated that annual sales of camping vehicles increased by 400 per cent during the sixties and reports a rising preference for the more elaborate and more costly units.[12]

"All indications are that the over-all leisure market will keep on growing. We believe that it will reach $250 billion by 1975. What is more, we believe that leisure will be the dynamic element in the domestic economy in the 1970's and that it will even out perform the economy."

From a report prepared in 1968 by Merrill Lynch, Pierce, Fenner, and Smith, Incorporated.

Not only have many long-established corporations diversified their activity to enter the expanding markets for leisure products, but they have also established employee recreation programs which have added further acceleration toward a leisure-oriented society. More than 50,000 companies now have some kind of recreation program for their employees and their families and more than 8,000 of these employ recreation directors. Between 1960 and 1970, corporations increased their investment in employee recreation programs from $1 billion to $2.5 billion per year.[13]

6. *Improved systems of communication and transportation.*

Included among the leisure industries, of course, but deserving special consideration are the electronic media and the travel systems. A television set can be found in more than 95 per cent of American homes. (One-fourth of these homes have two or more sets.) Already a major influence upon personal, family and social behavior, television will probably continue to expand its role in the future as cartridge programming and cable networks reach full development. Besides television sets, Americans are adequately fortified with radios, having one currently in use for every man, woman and child in the country. Suffering a decline as a result of the advent of television, motion pictures have now made their comeback and are drawing larger audiences each year.[14]

Along with developments in electronic communication have come developments in travel that have caught the fancy of more and more Americans. Travel by airplane and by automobile has become especially attractive, and spending for pleasure travel has reached the rate of $40 billion per year as compared with only $20 billion in 1960.[15] Special youth fares have made airplane travel highly attractive to young people resulting in a fantastic increase in the numbers of young Americans sight-seeing and studying abroad. More than three-quarters of a million Americans under the age of thirty visited Britain in 1971. Travel agents predict that six and a half million Americans will visit Europe in 1972.

It is impossible to assess the scope or the significance of the developments in modern communication and transportation as far as the values and life styles of the American people are concerned, but there can be little doubt that these are making an impact upon both our personal development and our social patterns.

7. Broader programs of health, education and welfare.

Since the end of World War II, American society has steadily increased its investments in health care,

in education, and in economic security. These investments have come from both private and public sectors
and have resulted in greatly expanded economic and
social opportunities for all Americans, including the
old and the young, the rich and the poor, the self-
sufficient and the dependent. For those who have been
affected by these developments, the abundance and
quality of life, including the possibilities for leisure,
have vastly improved.

In the past, much of the motivation for health, education and welfare programs has been based upon the
desire to increase economic productivity. In the future,
the major stimulus will be the desire to enhance enjoyment and meaning of human life.

8. Increase governmental participation.

Federal, State and City governments have been
among the chief agents of the leisure revolution. In
fact, without governmental participation, many of the
most significant aspects of that revolution could not
have appeared. Outdoor recreation, for example, depends heavily upon the 234 million acres (roughly
one-eighth of the total land area of the U.S.) which
have been set aside and managed by various levels of
government. These governments spend more than a
billion dollars a year to maintain these lands for recreational use.

State governments spent nearly $30 million in 1969
to attract tourists to their areas, an increase of 28.2%
in three years. The State of Hawaii spent nearly two

million, while New York, Texas, Georgia, Pennsylvania, South Carolina, Virginia, Michigan, Kentucky, and North Carolina each spent more than one million.[16]

Government contracts and subsidies have also played an important role in the development of the communication and transportation industries. Governments are also the major providers for health care and education, as well as assistance to the economically dependent. On a very limited basis, but one which is almost certain to expand, governments have been involved in the sponsorship of cultural arts programs, often subsidizing the efforts of private groups.

In any event, the positive role of government at various levels must be recognized as a major force among the trends toward a leisure-oriented society. Furthermore, it is to be expected that governments' role will be increased as the direction and dynamics of that society becomes more clearly discernible.

9. Increasing emphasis upon personal freedom.

The economic and educational system of American society were developed around the principle of deferred rewards. "Work now, play later," "Save for a rainy day," and "Learn it well and you'll learn to appreciate it someday," were part of the folk wisdom on which generations of Americans have been reared. Furthermore, there has been a strong tendency in American evangelical religion to equate pleasure with sin.

Many still cannot enjoy pleasure without feelings of

guilt, but the engines of the American economy, especially mass-media advertising, have been creating an increasing demand for immediate gratification. "Fly now, pay later" has become our new motto and our vast system of installment credit makes this economically possible.

Paralleling the economic encouragements toward immediate gratification have been various social movements which have focused attention upon human freedom and fulfillment. The civil rights movement, the student protests, and women's liberation have all aroused demands and desires for social changes to enhance personal freedom and opportunity. Add to these the rise of continuing education, the human potential movement, the do-it-yourself movement, Dr. Spock, the Playboy Philosophy, and a wide variety of other social phenomena of the past quarter century. The total effect of all of these diverse movements and trends is the emergence of a society that allows and encourages its members to seek satisfaction here and now rather than wait for some future reward.

The drive for personal freedom and fulfillment has been accelerated by what Theodore Levitt has called a "silent revolt" against the impersonal system of modern society and the mass production quality of modern life. Levitt claims that the rapid rise of many of the so-called leisure industries can be explained in terms of the need for outlets for individual expression and accomplishment—a need which was traditionally fulfilled through work but which often goes unfilled in the corporate work structures of society today.

The skier, the golfer, and the painter are each engaged in a solitary activity whose credit for mastery will be uncontestably his own, unshared by others and not lost deep in the bowels of some cooperating task force or team.[17]

10. Mounting skepticism concerning traditional economic values and social institutions.

To some Americans, however, especially many members of the younger generation, a "silent revolt" is not enough. As far as they are concerned, the American technocracy is not hospitable to human development. Some have already renounced their citizenship in that technocracy and have committed their lives to the making of a "counter-culture," i.e. an alternative society with social values and structures which are often directly antithetical to those of the established culture and calculated to ultimately subvert them.[18]

Others affirm our technology progress, but insist that it calls for new political and social forms. These forms will grow out of a new consciousness of what it means to be human and to participate in a society committed to human interests. This new consciousness has been heralded by many, but its most confident and flamboyant treatment has been provided by Charles Reich in *The Greening of America:*

> There is a revolution coming. It will not be like revolutions of the past. It will originate with the individual and with culture, and it will change the political structure only as its final act.... It is now spreading with amazing rapidity, and already our laws, institutions and social structure are changing in

consequence. It promises a higher reason, a more human community, and a new and liberated individual. . . .[19]

Addressing the First General Assembly of the World Future Society in May, 1971, author and corporate consultant Ian H. Wilson predicted that the changes in attitudes and values about which Reich and others have written will result in as much "groaning" of America as "greening." He nevertheless affirms the reality of a "New Reformation" in the values and goals of western civilization and urges that this phenomena be understood as more than a movement of impatient and presumptuous youth.

> For society as a whole, the major implications of these trends is that the seventies will be a decade of questioning, uncertainty, potential turmoil and confrontation. There will be substantial restructuring of many institutions; an effort to re-think their social purpose and objectives and reshape their operations and relationships, both internal and external. For business in particular, there will be the need to face up to the consequences of real questioning, challenge and modification of many basic business concepts — growth, technology, efficiency, profit, work, the legitimacy and authority of management.[20]

We will say more about "new consciousness" and "new reformation" in another chapter. The point which is intended here is simply that traditional economic values and their related social institutions are being challenged, not only by young radicals and the "counter culture" but also by many committed members of the American corporate structure.

Summary

These ten trends provide our profile of the "leisure revolution." In a sense, they are ten revolutions, since each one has its own dynamic or developmental process and each one will have its own impact upon personal life styles and social values. But, more important, they are all related and together constitute a much larger and pervasive revolution—a revolution that defies single-track study, and short-ranged interpretations.

By the "leisure revolution," therefore, we mean a conglomerate of contemporary trends affecting nearly every aspect of American society during the second half of the twentieth century. The "leisure revolution" involves those who work, as well as those who cannot or will not work, in the modern corporate system. It involves the young and the old, the rich and the poor, the informed and the ignorant. Women and children are as involved as men; the home is affected as much as the factory; the school is as crucial as the legislative halls. Our work, our play and our worship are all being reshaped. Our sense of who we are and what we are doing with life is exposed and our ways of relating to each other are being transformed.

We may be tempted to dismiss, or attempt to subvert, some of these trends in the interest of protecting our *status quos,* but such an attitude is futile and self-defeating. It would be naive to face these trends with unqualified enthusiasm, but in general they can be affirmed and celebrated since they represent new surges of human freedom and fulfillment. Whatever their meaning, regarded singly or in conglomerate, they can hardly be ignored by any contemporary American Christian. In fact, unless we relate to these trends creatively and compassionately, the rest of the world—including our Christian brothers—will condemn us for our arrogance and stupidity.

4

The Rise and Fall
of the Work-Ethic

It may seem strange, but in an attempt to illuminate the relationship between the religious attitudes and the economic behavior of Americans in the latter half of the twentieth century, we will rely heavily upon the writings of three nineteenth century Europeans—Karl Marx, Max Weber, and Alexis de Tocqueville.[1]

It was Karl Marx, of course, who first claimed that the economic interests and values of a people determine their social, political and even religious ideology. It was Max Weber who demonstrated that while economic interests may indeed influence religious attitudes, the reverse is also most certainly visible in the history of modern societies. And it was Alexis de Tocqueville who first observed that regardless of the diverse national and religious ancestry of nineteenth century

Americans, they shared a common democratic religion characterized by an intense dedication to productive work and an almost unshakable confidence in its salubrious and sanctifying possibilities for both themselves and their posterity.

When we speak of a work-ethic, therefore, we are talking about a concept which is both a product of our historical development and one which is comprised of both religious and economic ingredients. (Likewise, in another chapter, we will see that the leisure-ethic is also the result of historical process and consists of a mixture of religious and economic factors.)

The Work-ethic Defined

To begin with, let us be clear about what we mean by the work-ethic. It has been called several things and has various shades of meaning—depending upon how religious or how secular a definition is sought. Basically, however, the work-ethic consists of two elements: The first is that a man's work, i.e. his job, his occupation, his craft, his profession or whatever he does that pays off in terms of money or its equivalent is the most important aspect of his life and takes precedence over all other aspects. The second is that each man will be rewarded for his work, but he must not seek to enjoy that reward until his work is finished. When we refer to the work-ethic, therefore, we will be focusing upon these two elements—the notion of the primacy of work and the notion of deferred reward.

The Biblical Background

In his classic essay, *The Protestant Ethic and the Spirit of Capitalism,* Max Weber points out that there is no biblical basis for the so-called Protestant ethic from which the modern work-ethic has evolved. The biblical peoples were hard-working peoples, to be sure, and their literature is laced with admonitions concerning work, but nowhere in Scripture is a man's worldly work either exalted as the primacy aspect of life or offered as a basis for future rewards. The Bible, in fact, leans heavily in the opposite direction in that it often suggests that man's work in the world gets in the way of his salvation.

In the creation story, for example, work appears as the sign of man's demotion and banishment, certainly not the mark of his nobility, nor the seat of virtue, nor the source of his hope.[2] The history of Israel shows that its religious life revolved around periods of abstinence from work and that the Israelites were repeatedly reminded that it was not by their human achievements, but by their trust in God's promises, that their destiny would be fulfilled. Their "holy-days" were frequent and they were all observed by strict prohibitions against regular work.[3]

Nor was Jesus a very good model for a work-ethic. He not only left his own work as a carpenter, but he called countless others away from their jobs also and preached again and again about the spiritual hazards of becoming too preoccupied with worldly work and the pursuit of wealth and power.[4] As Sebastian de Grazia has noted:

> Early Christianity kept well in mind what Jesus Christ had said about the birds of the air: "They sow not, neither do they reap nor gather into barns; yet your Heavenly Father feedeth them. Are you not much better than they?" Christians were not to waste their time thinking, planning, and working for the morrow. . . . For the patristic age the end was salvation, the other life. The first thing was to save one's soul, to bring it closer to God. Work, in a sense, was something one did in his free time. . . .[5]

The Medieval Roman Catholic Church

The disdain of the early Christians for the things of this world and their eagerness to prepare for the kingdom of God eventually led to the medieval Catholic doctrines which bifurcated human affairs into sacred and secular categories. Religious elitism also developed, separating those who took vows of exclusive dedication to spiritual work from those who continued to work at the ordinary tasks of life. A notion of *vocatio* emerged to declare that the primary purpose of a Christian's life was to offer special spiritual works unto God—to pray, to meditate, to withdraw from the concerns of this life and embrace a discipline which actively suppressed the interests of the flesh. Those who embraced this *vocatio* were inducted into a special religious caste and often retired to special communities where they could concentrate on their holy work with a minimum of worldly distraction.

The medieval church developed strong moral teachings against avarice and usury and even those who did not take the vows of total dedication were expected to refrain from striving for personal gain. The church itself became a powerful economic force and many of its members engaged in prosperous commercial activity, but secular work had spiritual significance only when its fruits were contributed to the church or to charity.

The Reformation: Martin Luther

Martin Luther attacked the medieval church's system of spiritual works as being both corrupted by men and unfaithful to Scripture. Luther argued that the so-called spiritual works were no better than ordinary work as far as God was concerned, but his primary point was that neither spiritual nor secular work contributes to salvation. Only the work of Christ merits salvation and men participate in that salvation by trusting in Christ's merit, not by their good works.

Luther, therefore, repudiated the notions of *vocatio* and offered instead the concept of *Beruf*. In *Beruf,* Luther combined two separate biblical concepts—the call to salvation by accepting God's free gift in Jesus Christ, and the admonition to remain steadfast in one's present responsibilities until the return of Christ.

As Weber and others have pointed out, Luther's concept of *Beruf* combined the call to salvation by grace through faith with the call to earthly obedience and service, but it did not establish a causal relationship between the two callings. Faith, for Luther, was demonstrated by the diligent use of the Word and the Sacraments, not by significant or successful human achievement.[6]

John Calvin and the Puritans

Although Luther's theology played a pivotal role by undermining the church's system of spiritual works, it was really the theology of John Calvin that provided the foundations for the modern work-ethic. Extending Luther's argument that it is God's work, not the work of men that accomplishes salvation, Calvin declared that God has already determined the destinies of all men. Some he has predestined for salvation and these shall surely be saved; others he has predestined for damnation and these shall indeed be damned. Nothing can change a man's destiny—neither works, nor sacraments, nor holy days, nor priests, nor the power of the church, nor anything else.

Along with his doctrine of predestination, however, Calvin also gave his followers a concept of Christian calling that differed from both the Catholic *vocatio* and Luther's *Beruf*. Calvin taught that men are called, neither to spiritual exercises nor to quiet acceptance of grace, but to actively glorify God in the work. The Calvinists took themselves very seriously as the stewards of God's creation, which meant among other things that they sought to improve its rather dilapidated state. The most militant of the Calvinists thus became known as Puritans and each one had his own special role, or "calling," through which he glorified God in a direct and personal way.

Although the doctrine of predestination taught the Puritan that there was nothing he could do to accomplish his salvation, the Calvinist notion of calling provided him with at least a basis for discerning whether or not he was among the elect. Since God has promised to bless those whom he has determined to save and threatened to torment those whom he has damned, one ought to be able to find some hints about his destiny in the way he is faring in this life—especially in his calling. If one is prospering in his calling, it must indeed be that he is enjoying the blessing of God which, of course, suggests that he is among the elect. On the other hand, if one has no calling—or is floundering in a calling—that can only mean that he is experiencing a foretaste of things to come.

For the Puritans, therefore, secular work took on profound spiritual significance. They knew they could not earn salvation by their work, but they had no other basis upon which to assess their spiritual condition nor any other means of expressing their religious devotion. It became a matter of religious necessity that every aspect of their lives, as well as every aspect of their social and natural environment, be brought under the discipline of rational control and development. While Catholics, Lutherans, and the evangelical sects could experience an assurance of salvation through occasional flourishes of piety, a faithful Puritan was subject to a lifetime of systematic self-improvement and a desperate quest for worldly success lest his earthly life show the symptoms of being bound for hell. This dedication to self-improvement and success became the Puritan's ethic, or as Weber called it, the Protestant ethic.

The Secularization of the Protestant Ethic

Although the Protestant ethic enabled the Puritans to participate most actively in the development of modern capitalism and in the establishment of American institutions, its religious dimensions were eventually overshadowed by economic, political, and social considerations. Successive generations became less and less interested in its theological origins and more and more interested in its practical utility.

In the process of secularization, however, the Calvinist understanding of the relationship between salvation and earthly success actually became reversed. An orthodox Calvinist, for example, would insist that earthly success is a consequence of being destined to salvation; the secularized Puritan, however, tended to view salvation as the consequence of earthly success. In that shift, the Protestant ethic of the seventeenth and eighteenth centuries became what nineteenth and twentieth century men know as the work-ethic. One needs only to read the works of such founding fathers as Thomas Jefferson and Benjamin Franklin to see how the morality and institutions of Puritanism were able to thrive in the New World without necessarily clinging to their European theological foundations.

When the French aristocrat, Alexis de Tocqueville, visited the United States in the 1840s, he noted that

On my arrival in the United States, the religious aspect of the country was the first thing that struck my attention; and the longer I stayed there, the more I perceived the great political consequences resulting from this...." [7]

By the "religious aspect," however, Tocqueville meant something more than the plethora of religious sects and the flurry of religious activity which were visible to this cosmopolitan tourist. What caught his attention was the fact that, in spite of their ethnic and religious diversity, the Americans shared a common religious spirit and were well on their way toward developing a common democratic religion—a religion characterized by a belief in the ultimate perfectability of man and his society and by a devotion to work as the means of achieving that perfection.

After observing its influence in American society, Tocqueville was convinced that a social ethic based upon the meritorious and salubrious significance of work was the key to the success of any democratic society. He recognized that the work-ethic which energized and disciplined the Americans had been grounded in their religious tradition, but he believed that religion alone could not, and should not, sustain that ethic. In fact, noting that the temporal power of religious institutions had been on the wane since the Middle Ages, Tocqueville prophesied an increasing role for secular governments in the promulgation of this doctrine:

Governments must apply themselves to restore to men that love of the future with which religion...(can) no longer inspire them; and, without saying so, they must practically teach the community day by day that wealth, fame, and power are the rewards of labor, that great success stands at the utmost range of long desire, and that there is nothing lasting but what is obtained by toil.[8]

Perhaps no man in history, therefore, could have been more pleased than Alexis de Tocqueville to hear an American President address his people 125 years later with the words:

Let the detractors of America, the doubters of the American spirit, take note. America's competitive spirit, the work-ethic of this people, is alive and well on Labor Day, 1971. The dignity of work, the value of achievement, the morality of self-reliance — none of these is going out of style.[9]

The Demise of the Work-ethic in American Society

Alexis de Tocqueville and Richard Nixon notwithstanding, the work-ethic has lost its grip upon American society and neither the persuasion of organized religion nor the pressure of omnipresent government will restore its influence. The work-god is dead and the morality which has been sustained for generations by the worship of work is being renounced more emphatically every day. There are many pious and patriotic Americans who refuse to believe that any change has taken place, and there are those, like Richard Nixon, who cling to hopes that the gospel of work can still regain its lost prestige and power, but the realities of

American economic and social life today militate against such hopes.

Ironically, it is not the failure of the work-ethic that has been its undoing, but its success. Propelled by their worship of work, Americans have created such a splendid system of material abundance and technological wonders that they simply cannot resist the temptation to enjoy it! In fact, the continued momentum of their economy is contingent upon their expanding capacity to consume all the goods and gadgets they have worked so hard to produce.

At the beginning of this chapter, we pointed out that the work-ethic consisted of two basic elements— the notion that a man's work (his job, or occupation, or profession) is the most important aspect of his life (and must therefore take precedence over all other aspects) and the notion that the rewards for working are to be deferred until the work is finished. It is now time to test the viability of that ethic against the realities of contemporary American economic life.

Work is still necessary and good, but it has never been a legitimate end in itself. Even the hard-working Puritans saw work, not as an end, but as a means—in their case a means of glorifying God or confirming their election. Even among our more secular forebears, work was conceived as means to an end—whether the end be that of private prosperity or of public progress. As Tocqueville noted, however, work was a *necessary* means to almost any noble or worthy end to which members of a democratic society might aspire. There was simply no way that any American could attain comfort, security and status except through his work. Nor was there any alternative but to wait for his reward. In other words, both of the notions which formed the basis for the work-ethic were reinforced by the realities of economic life for those generations which espoused that ethic.

For an American of Richard Nixon's generation to espouse the work-ethic, however, requires a leap of faith that defies contemporary economic realities. Not only is there a shortage of opportunities to work in the narrow sense of a job or occupation, but there are ever increasing portions of American society which are being offered alternatives to work. It is too simplistic to say that men are being replaced by machines as far as work is concerned, but technology has so changed the character and meaning of work that even those who spend most of their time and energy at work have become increasingly aware that it cannot be the primary source of their life's meaning and values.

And then there are the millions of Americans who, for a wide variety of reasons, are not working—the youth who are in schools and colleges, the aging who have retired from work, the unskilled who cannot find jobs, those who are physically and mentally unable to work, and those who simply choose not to work. At one time, the American economy needed more of these non-working members of society as producers; today it needs them more as consumers. Basically, this means that they have to have economic power for which they have not worked. (But what an affront this is to those who espouse the work-ethic!) Beyond the bare dynamics of production and consumption, however, modern Americans are searching desperately for a scheme of meanings and values that will bring poignancy and quality into their lives. Work has brought them comfort, security and status, but they are discovering that they want more from life than what their work can offer. Some, especially among the young, have rejected the work system altogether as a source of meaning and purpose for life. Most want to work, but they do not want to make work the center of their lives.

Furthermore, the notion of deferred rewards has become economically disfunctional in American society. For better or for worse, our economy is sustained by our systems of credit. Waiting until we could pay cash was once sound principle; today it is almost subversive. "Work now, play later" has been replaced by "Fly now, pay later."

In other words, neither of the two basic elements of the work-ethic are sustained by contemporary economic realities. On the one hand, our continued economic development demands that more and more Americans find more and more outlets for self-expression and enjoyment apart from working at jobs. And on the other, our credit-based economy requires that we consume the goods and services we produce as soon and as quickly as possible. You might say that our economy operates on a principle of "no deposit—no return." For a hundred years its expansion came through the translation of raw materials into finished products. Today, its expansion depends upon speeding the flow of goods from the assembly line to the trash heap. Our biggest economic problem consists of finding new ways to put money into the hands of those who are not getting any or enough from working in order that they, too, might consume their fair share of goods and services. From a strictly economic point of view, it is almost irrelevant whether or not they obtain this money by working.

What has happened in American society to bring about such a drastic shift in economic values? Who has subverted the cherished virtues? Who can be blamed for the demise of those doctrines of Christian economics which made our nation great?

Well, we could blame the youth. After all, it is the younger generation that is most flagrantly flaunting its scorn of the work-ethic. But who is it that bought them all their toys? Who decided that they should spend their formative years in schools rather than at jobs? Who created the conditions which have enabled them to become the first leisure class that American society has produced? Who? Their parents, of course. Their hard-working, quiet living parents—in many cases, parents who have been so conditioned by work-ethic that they have felt guilty about enjoying life themselves so they have tried to enjoy it vicariously through their children.

The efforts of parents to impose a leisure oriented society upon their offspring have been greatly reinforced by the engines of the American economy—especially the mass-media. Nearly every industry has tried to cultivate the youth market. The direct economic power of youth is minimal, but their indirect power is enormous—and the advertisers know it. Those who are steeped in the virtues of work and suspicious of play cannot be easily persuaded to spend their hard-earned money on playthings for themselves, but they will gladly buy them for their sons and daughters. It is no wonder, therefore, that the advertisers address their message to youth—those who have not yet been conditioned to the values of work nor made any commitments to the systems of work and yet have money to spend.

And what is the content of that message to youth? That life revolves around work? That money should be saved? That temptation to indulge in the pleasures of life should be avoided? Far from it! The message is that life revolves around leisure activities and leisure goods, that money is to be spent before it is even earned, and that pleasure is to be pursued.

It is this discrepancy between the espoused values and actual practice of their parents, and the contradiction between the established doctrines of our economic system and the images projected by the mass media, that have caused much of the so-called generation gap. As Sebastian de Grazia has noted, youth feel betrayed by their parents and the established systems at the very same time they are being indulged by them. They see their parents' worship of work as a cruel hypocrisy. They see the work orientation of the educational establishment as a deception. Their own experience as a leisure class, their own exposure to the media, and often their own parents' hurried and worried, work oriented life styles convince them that work is essentially bad, rather than good, and that the way to the good life will be the one that involves the least work.[10]

It is impossible to predict, of course, how contemporary American youth and young adults will feel about work in their later years, but it is doubtful that they will embrace the work-ethic any more firmly in their future. The economic conditions of American society are not apt to become any more hospitable to the notions which undergirded the work-ethic. Nor would appeals to traditional religious and national doctrines seem to promise any great influence upon a generation which has found that it can live quite comfortably with minimal loyalties to church and state.

Shorter work weeks, longer vacations, earlier retirement, and an increasing flow of material goods are significant economic trends, but they do not in themselves constitute a revolution. Richard Nixon, and most of his generation will go to their graves believing in both the beneficence of these ecomonic trends and in the eternal and universal validity of the work-ethic. They have become rightly disturbed about some of the things they see in the younger generation, however, because it is the peculiar role which is being played by American youth which is transforming the seemingly benign economic trends into a revolution.

In describing the conditions which were producing a new industrial social order a hundred years ago, Karl Marx pointed out that when men began to leave their homes in pursuit of their livelihood and especially when they become congregated in factories, they developed a class-consciousness as workers and became a revolutionary force within traditional pre-industrial systems — a force which, according to Marx, would eventually lead to their rule of the industrial state.

De Grazia has suggested that in the post-war period a similar phenomenon has occurred among American youth. By sending our youth away to school and to jobs in the city, by congregating them in colleges and young adult ghettos, and by cultivating them as a market for leisure activities and leisure goods via the mass media, we have given them a class consciousness as youth or young adults and they have developed their own cultural forms, their own value systems and their own life styles. Because these values and life styles revolve around their leisure more than their work, we may even call this a *leisure* class consciousness.[11]

During this same period some of the weaknesses of the American system have become more visible. Racism, poverty, militarism, pollution, sexism, etc., are not new in American society—what is new is their public exposure. Youth have been quick to exploit these conditions as weaknesses of the American system and failures of previous generations. They have thus developed a sense of self-confidence, indeed a sense of self-righteousness, at a time when increasing numbers of older Americans have begun questioning their faith in the traditional systems and values of American society.

It is quite possible, therefore (and the indications are rampant) that during the seventies American society will find its youth mounting a frontal assault upon the traditional American work-ethic analogous to the attack on the war-ethic which was waged by youth in the sixties. This does not mean that work is passing away or that youth are necessarily repudiating its necessity or value. It means, however, that they no longer regard work as the primary element in personal life style or social values and they are concluding that the postponement of its rewards promotes frustration rather than piety.

5

Leisure Is More than Time Away from Work

There is a story about a traveler who approached a local resident asking directions for getting to a certain destination. "Oh yes, I know where that is," responded the resident, "that will be easy to find." But when he started to give directions, he became confused. What had seemed so simple appeared to get more and more complicated as he tried to explain it to the stranger. Finally, in exasperation he said, "Well, I guess you can't get there from here."

This story suggests something about the plight of those who are trying to find or give directions towards a moral and spiritual understanding of leisure. Indeed, there are many Christians who are finding themselves "strangers" looking for some direction in a leisure-oriented society and there have been various attempts to offer guidance which have proven unsuccessful.

In fact, there are even some efforts to convince the churches that they should be mobilizing for a return to more familiar territory by resuscitating the gods of Hard Work and Deferred Rewards.

The problem with most of the efforts to develop a Christian understanding of leisure (and with most so-called leisure ministries) is that they have usually started from conventional notions about leisure — notions which have arisen out of recent experience with economic and social trends but which have been rarely subjected to any philosophical or theological reflection. Like everyone else, for example, Christian ministers and laymen have been thinking and talking about leisure as "free time." Like everyone else, they have understood leisure primarily in terms of its juxtaposition to work — as rest or reward from work. And like nearly everyone else, they have attempted to program leisure with various forms of entertainment and distraction — constructive entertainment, to be sure, sometimes even *creative* entertainment, but entertainment, nevertheless.

As a result, there are still no clear directions toward a Christian understanding of leisure. There are sincere and significant efforts in several denominations, but there are also those who have quietly admitted, "Well, I guess you can't get there from here."

The first step, therefore, towards a Christian understanding of leisure must be one of conceptual reconstruction. The leisure revolution has exploded conventional notions about leisure at the same time that it has shattered the traditional values of work. It is forcing a search for fresh definitions and descriptions. The purpose of this chapter is to combine some contemporary observations with some theological reflections in order to begin the development of an adequate conceptual vocabulary with which to understand, communicate, and ultimately evaluate, the encounter between Christian faith and the leisure revolution.

What leisure is NOT

For openers, let us make a frontal attack on the three most popular notions about leisure to be found in American society (including the churches) today:

1. Leisure is not free time.

Conventional notions about leisure are usually bound to categories of time. Leisure is often equated with free time, meaning, in most cases, time which is free from work.

To think of leisure as free time, however, is false and misleading. Leisure means freedom, to be sure, but freedom cannot be chopped up into chunks of time. Besides, many people experience their greatest freedom when they are working and some are anything but free when they are cut off from their work.

Free time is an alien and spurious notion to any Christian who reflects theologically upon the details and dynamics of his life. On the one hand, to a Christian *all* of his time is free — his life has been given and redeemed by God apart from any work on his own part. Life is a gift, given freely by God and intended to be received and shared freely by his people when they are at work as well as when they are at play. On the other hand, *none* of a Christian's time is free time in the sense that he is free to do anything he pleases with it. It is all committed to God — whether it is being spent working or playing. In his writings about Christian freedom, Luther described a Christian as one who always lives in both total freedom and total responsibility. He cannot divide his life into neat segments thinking that sometimes he is free and at other times he is not free.

The notion of free time also militates against responsible participation in our complex society. It assumes that a man's work is his only real responsibility and that other responsibilities are optional. Free time suggests that when a man is not working, he can spend his time doing anything he pleases. This is neither possible nor desirable in our complex corporate society with its increasing interdependence. Indeed, many people today, especially people who are alert and active citizens, are finding that they simply have no such thing as free time. They may be spending less time working at their jobs, but they are busy with other responsibilities and often find too little time to do all that they feel that they should. Because leisure is so often equated with free time, they conclude that they have no leisure. "Leisure?" they ask cynically, "Who has any of that these days?" Because they have an inadequate and misleading concept of what leisure is all about, they fail to see how their lives are being affected by the leisure revolution.

Probably the only people in American society who have any abundance of free time are those who are in some sense removed from active participation, such as those who are hospitalized or imprisoned and perhaps some of those who have been involuntarily disemployed or retired. It is cruel irony to call their situation free, however, and it certainly cannot be considered leisure.

2. Leisure is not rest or reward from work.

Most Americans approach leisure with the residual moralism of their Puritan and Rationalist heritage. That is, as we have already discussed in the first chapter, they tend to make work, not only the center of their lives, but also the reference point for all other aspects.

The Puritans saw men as stewards of God's creation, each of whom had some special calling at which he should work diligently and productively. The Rationalists saw men as the conscious components of a vast and intricate rational universe, each man having a function in its continued operation. In both the religious and the secular cosmologies which have dominated the development of American thought, man was conceived as *homo faber,* man the worker, and his primary role was to labor at his particular place in the system.[1]

Whether or not they affirm these cosmologies, modern men cling to the self-understandings and roles which these cosmologies assigned. (That is, modern middle-class whites cling to them; minorities, the poor, and many of the young see themselves differently.) Most of the systems of American society, especially the economic and educational systems, have been built upon the eternal and universal validity of the *homo faber* notions.

The problem with the concepts of *homo faber* is that they have obscured and stifled our understanding of *homo ludens,* man the player. If work, and work alone, is the central function of human existence, then there is no role for play — and any form of idleness is suspect unless it can be justified in terms of work. The Puritans and Rationalists played and rested, but they conceived their play and rest as preparation or refreshment or reward for work. There was no place for any frivolity and they had little appreciation for contemplation — unless, of course, it was clearly aimed at purifying the mind for more dedicated and disciplined service. Even their games, sports and hobbies reflected their orientation to work in the sense that they usually were exercises designed to develop physical and mental skills that would be useful in work.

Leisure enhances work in a variety of ways, but when it is seen as the servant of work, or has to derive its significance from work, it soon loses its quality and poignancy. How quickly, for example, the joy and excitement of learning can disappear when the learning is regimented into assigned lessons. Or, how easily an act of courtesy or kindness becomes deflated when it is either demanded, or is offered with the expectation of compensation. Unless there is meaning and value in the experience itself, apart from any significance in relationship to work, it will not have the freedom or the authentic self-expression which makes it truly leisure — and appreciation of the experience will be diminished.

The notion that leisure derives its only meaning from work is responsible for the rise of three serious neuroses among contemporary Americans. Symptoms of these neuroses are abundant everywhere, including almost every congregation. (In fact, they are sometimes found to be flourishing abundantly in the manse!)

Work Addiction

The most rampant of these neuroses (and perhaps the most difficult to cure) is *work addiction*. For those who cannot appreciate leisure for its own sake, only work has real meaning and value. They may agree that other things, including even play, are all right in small doses, but they will insist that it is really only their work which is fulfilling to themselves and contributing to society. So they invest more and more of themselves in their work — and become increasingly dependent upon it. Their work becomes their god — before whom shall come no other gods (nor for that matter, other men). Medical reports do not provide statistics on the numbers of people suffering from work addiction, but medical authorities have come to recognize this neurosis as a primary factor in many other ailments for which statistics abound!

THE EXODUS COMPLEX

The second, and almost equally wide-spread, neurosis of modern work-oriented Americans might be called the *exodus complex*. This is the compulsive pursuit of freedom from everyday routine. Since work for most Americans is pretty ordinary, then those for whom leisure is defined in terms of work search for it in the extraordinary. Since work ties them down, then leisure must take them away! Since work tends to become dull, then leisure must be sought in new thrills — perhaps even violent thrills! The exodus complex is the contemporary American's need to keep moving, to be always going somewhere — anywhere — to get away from it all. It is the flight for freedom — and it is usually scheduled to depart at 4:30 Friday afternoon.

JUSTIFIABLE SUICIDE

The third neurosis could be called *justifiable suicide*. It afflicts primarily those who become so obsessed with the virtues of earning a living that they become easy prey to its vices — i.e., those who are so proud of the fact that they are working so hard that they can hardly wait to reward themselves by indulging every urge to eat, drink, and make payments. This neurosis is generally not as easily discerned as work addiction or the exodus complex, but its symptoms can be diagnosed whenever someone says something like "I earned it, so by golly I'm going to enjoy it," or, perhaps something like "I'm going to get my share of the fun out of life, even if it kills me." (And it often does.)

These three contemporary ailments all spring from the conception that the meaning and value of leisure comes from its relationship to work. It is little wonder, therefore, that those who suffer from these neuroses never seem to experience any real leisure, but simply burn themselves out trying to work harder and play harder.

The American economic system is a many splendored thing. It enables the average American to enjoy a standard of living that his forefathers (and the vast majority of his contemporaries around the world) could scarcely imagine. Being an American means having access to more goods and services than he can possibly use or enjoy in his lifetime.

Because the American economic system depends upon ever-accelerating rates of production and consumption, however, Americans are caught on a treadmill of working and consuming. The harder they work, the more they are enabled and encouraged to consume. The more they consume, the harder they must work. Ours is the only society in the history of civilization that offers its people the choice of working themselves to death or consuming themselves to death, or both.

Unless Americans can be educated away from their orgy of production and consumption, they may well destroy themselves, their environment, and perhaps their planet. But as long as leisure is understood as merely the counterpart of work, there is no chance of breaking the vicious cycle.

3. Leisure is not simply constructive entertainment or distraction.

Some people conceive of leisure as a primarily passive experience and expect to realize it by merely switching to the right channel, or finding the right hobby, or perhaps simply waiting for something (or someone) to come along and turn them on. This notion seems to prevail especially among those who invest nearly all of their energy and interest in their work, so they have little to bring or give to a leisure experience. Their quest for leisure then becomes a search for entertainment — and it often ends in mere time-filling (or time-killing) distractions.

Entertainment can be very enjoyable and refreshing, but few people can live on entertainment alone or can find any freedom in a routine of work and distraction. Human beings need to be actively engaged — with one another and with their times — or they cease to be human, and their engagement must be a meaningful one, not merely one that fills (or kills) time. As the great jurist Oliver Wendell Holmes once said, "As life is action and passion, it is required of a man that he should share the passion and action of his time, at peril of being judged not to have lived." [2]

Work has traditionally filled the need for engagement for most people and, hopefully, will continue to engage men meaningfully. But work alone cannot and should not comprise the totality of their participation in the life of the world — and there are increasing numbers of people who simply have no work in which they can find any sense of engagement or fulfillment. Are we willing to settle for life styles that merely alternate working at a meaningless job and being distracted by inane entertainments? Have we no better understanding of the creativity and dignity of human beings, especially our senior citizens and our handicapped or disemployed members, than to assume that their needs are filled when they are provided with economic security and entertainment? If not, we have become as crass and shortsighted as those Romans who allowed their civilization to crumble because they thought human and social needs could be satisfied with bread and circuses.

The notion that leisure is primarily entertainment with which to fill or kill time leads to disillusionment and despair. Woe be unto those churchmen who think of leisure, or attempt to develop leisure ministries, primarily in terms of programming the time of people with activities that merely entertain or distract them for awhile! There will always be a few who will respond to programming out of loyalty, curiosity, or sheer desperation, but the ultimate blow has been dealt to a person's dignity and pride when he is invited to merely "Come and enjoy yourself" (be entertained by our program), or "Let us teach you some interesting games" (which will help you forget that you are no longer really involved with the real world), or "Why don't you move into this beautiful place" (where you will be taken care of without any bother to anyone).

What, then, IS leisure?

Having assaulted the three most popular conceptions of leisure, it is now time to turn to a discussion of what leisure is really all about.

In the first place, it should be noted that the concept of leisure did not originate among twentieth century Americans but has its roots in classical antiquity. The Greeks and Romans had concepts of leisure which appear in the writings of their philosophers and poets. In every instance, leisure is understood and valued as a creative and liberating experience. The English word "leisure" is derived from the Latin *licere,* which means as a verb "to be permitted" and as a noun "the absence of restraint or coercion." The root meaning of "leisure," therefore, is "freedom" — not free time, or freedom from work, but simply freedom — without any reference to time or work.

Leisure means freedom, but not the kind of bloody freedom which results from the overthrow of a political oppressor, nor the kind of sweaty freedom that comes from defiance of social mores, nor the kind of teary freedom that accompanies abandoned commitments and broken relationships. Leisure is rather that sense of freedom which is realized when a person experiences more fully both his uniqueness and worth as an individual and his acceptance and relationship as part of the world around him. A person finds leisure when he discovers who he is, what he can do with his life, and what an abundance of happy circumstances and relationships in which his life is cast. A Christian experiences leisure when he comes into full awareness of the freedom he has in Christ, the freedom from fear and guilt because of sin but, even more important, the freedom to be and become the new man after Christ's own splendid example.

A leisure *revolution,* therefore, is more than just a complex variety of economic and social changes, however important (and they are important!) they might be. It is also a new shifting and surging of the spirit of Western civilization. New possibilities and problems, new roles and relationships, new values and life styles, new hopes and fears have arisen on every side. The most perceptive observers of contemporary American culture are writing about a new consciousness, a new mentality, and a new reformation and are describing changes which are occurring in the hearts and minds of men as well as changes in their society. Since all of these changes revolve around man's self-understanding and self-expression as a free agent in the universe, it is appropriate to collectively identify them, among other things, as a *leisure revolution.*

The leisure revolution does not necessarily mean that people are going to experience more free time, or that work is losing its importance, or that human life is becoming more passive. In fact, it may well mean the very opposite — that people are becoming busier than ever, that work is taking on greater dignity and significance, and that life will become much more active! (How absurd, therefore, the conventional notions about leisure have become.)

Traditional concepts of time and work are undergoing change and the values which have been assigned to them are being challenged. Fundamental questions concerning the meaning and style of human life are being asked and the traditional answers are being tested. Basic issues of economic process and social organization are being placed on the agenda for open debate. Ultimately, the leisure revolution means that American society is searching for ways of adequately appropriating its new opportunities for freedom — among its own citizens and throughout the rest of the world. If this search fails, our culture will either collapse in a monumental orgy of self-indulgence or ossify into technological totalitarianism!

To these brief definitions of leisure and leisure revolution, certain descriptive statements about the character of leisure might be added to construct a concept which will adequately convey its contemporary meaning.

1. Leisure is essentially spiritual, rather than economic or social, in character.

Leisure is the freedom that both allows and enables human beings to occasionally transcend the dimensions of economic and social necessity in which their lives are spent and participate in higher realities. It is a freedom that is more properly described as a partaking of eternity rather than as a particle of time. It should be discussed as free spirit rather than as free time.

Leisure affects the schedules and pocket books of men, but it affects their spirits more so. When people experience leisure, their spirits soar and their humanity finds larger expression. Without leisure, or with counterfeit leisure experiences, their spirits sag and they become dehumanized by either external or internal forces which gain control over them. The economic and social freedoms which have emerged in recent decades will mean little if they merely enable modern men to exchange familiar forms of bondage for new ones. If the freedom which is represented by leisure, therefore, is to be an authentic and enduring freedom, it must penetrate economic circumstances and social arrangements, however important those may be, and touch the souls of men and of their culture.

2. Leisure is a quality or style of life, rather than fragments of a lifetime.

Perhaps leisure would be better understood if only the adverbial form of the word, i.e., "leisurely," were used. "Leisurely" describes a style of life which is both theologically and sociologically appropriate for contemporary American Christians — theologically appropriate because they live by grace through faith in Jesus Christ and sociologically appropriate because they participate in a society of unprecedented abundance and opportunity.

Conceived as quality of life rather than as quantities of time, leisure requires no arbitrary distinctions between work and play, between that which is important or necessary and that which is unimportant or optional. Leisure can be experienced during times of work as well as times of play, in activity which is crucial as well as that which is frivolous. It will often mean freedom from work, at least freedom from the routines and requirements of work, but it need not be (and, indeed, should not be) juxtaposed against work as if they were experiences which were somehow incompatible. Work and play will shape the schedule of people's lives, but leisure provides the sense and style with which they go about it all.

The real significance of the leisure revolution, therefore, is not that it offers alternatives to work, but that it is liberating men from the meritorious meanings, as well as the production-oriented values, with which modern society has operated up to this point. Leisure, in other words, liberates men from their illusions of striving and myths of progress by enabling them to discover the presence of grace and peace in their daily walk. An adequate concept of leisure, therefore, involves an understanding of worship, as well as of work and play.

3. Leisure is man's synthesizing factor in a "component" civilization.

The rationalization of human experience which began with the Renaissance and Reformation and which has provided the framework for modern civilization is rapidly reaching the point of diminishing returns. Every aspect of the universe, including man himself, has been subjected to critical analysis and reduced to its constituent parts. As a result, men today are able to build machines that are nearly as complicated as persons (and many times more competent in performing mechanical and rational functions) and they are able to manipulate men nearly as well as they can operate machines.

In a sense, leisure offers men their only opportunity to escape being reduced to mere components of their technological systems. Some interpreters of technological civilization have already forecast the dehumanization and enslavement of men by technological systems and, as noted in an earlier chapter, several aspects of the "leisure revolution" are aimed squarely at shattering those scenarios — either by repudiating technology or by calling for new values by which to direct its development.[3]

In the first chapter, we noted that the primary elements of a Christian's life are his work, his play, and his worship. We suggested that most middle-class Americans have these elements confused — we worship our work, we work at our play, and we play at our worship — and are therefore missing much of the joy which is being offered by their freedom as Christians and their abundance as Americans. Furthermore, most Christians in America today are experiencing these elements as separate, often competing and conflicting, interests. In the context of that discussion, leisure means "getting it all together" in a new and better way — not by disparaging work in order to exalt play and get new kicks out of worship, but by inspiring in contemporary Christians a new consciousness of their freedom from many of the traditional worldly cares and concerns, offering them an abundance of alternatives for making their lives meaningful and pleasant, and challenging them to update their social systems and values in order to enable all human beings to enjoy *a full share of economic, social, and spiritual freedom.*

To summarize, therefore, this chapter has attempted to demonstrate that the conventional notions concerning leisure are inadequate for any Christian understanding or interpretation of the leisure revolution. Leisure today cannot be described as free time. It cannot be viewed as merely rest or reward from working. And it cannot be contained in programs of entertainment or distraction.

Instead, leisure must be understood as participation in a new surge of freedom, unlike (but not unrelated) to other surges of freedom which have recurred throughout the development of modern civilization. This freedom is essentially a spiritual experience, rather than an economic or social condition, but economic and social trends have nurtured (and been nurtured by) the spiritual experience. Leisure should be conceived as a qualitative, rather than a quantitative, aspect of human life, and its chief characteristic is its integrating and harmonizing function.

So much for the *concept* of leisure. In the next chapter, we will discuss its ethical and theological *context.*

6

The Emergence of a Leisure-Ethic and Its Implications for Christians Today

The evidence is fragmentary and ambiguous, but we are beginning to discern the emergence of a *leisure-ethic*.

This emerging new ethic is not altogether antithetical to the traditional work-ethic (nor is it likely to soon replace it), but it is already a viable alternative and is being consciously chosen by thousands of contemporary Americans—most of them young and many of them our most creative and committed Christians.

Like the work-ethic, the emerging leisure-ethic has both its significant religious and economic dimensions. That is, it is based upon certain understandings of man and his role in the cosmos and it is manifested in special forms of economic, social, and political behavior. It is part of what has been described as a "new consciousness," a "new mentality," and even a "new reformation," and its importance can no longer be ignored by either church or state.[1] In fact, the trauma of its emergence has already touched nearly every community in America, and it has been the seat of conflict in countless Christian homes and congregations.

The primary shapers and propagators of the leisure-ethic have thus far been largely youth and young adults — especially those offspring of hard-working, middle-class parents who have been caught up in the various liberation movements during the past decade and who have been experimenting with forms of counter-culture. If the leisure revolution is indeed part of a new reformation, then those students and other young people who have become angered and alienated by the established systems of American society are the "new Protestants," and the efforts to develop a counter-culture are the contemporary equivalent of the Calvinist theocracies of the sixteenth and seventeenth centuries. Ironically, their contempt for traditional (and perhaps decadent) Puritan values, together with their demand for greater individuality and more democratic social arrangements, have made the hippies the new Puritans. It is not surprising, therefore, that certain aspects of the new ethic are most clearly visible among the advocates and practitioners of counter-culture.

It would be short-sighted, however, to identify the emerging leisure-ethic exclusively with student protests, hippies, or counter-culture. Those students and other young adults who are solidly affirming the established system and taking full advantage of the opportunities for affluence, mobility, diversity, privacy and self-expression which it offers are doing as much to shape a leisure-ethic as those who are alienated — perhaps even more because they are usually not as hung up on ideological abstractions.

Nor is the new ethic confined to youth and young adults. There are many Americans at middle-age and mid-career, as well as thousands of senior citizens, who are joining the search for new meanings and values, experimenting with new life styles, and learning to celebrate leisure in their own way.

In fact, one of the most fascinating and hopeful aspects of the leisure-ethic is that it may somehow lead to a new unity and harmony within American society — even as the work-ethic provided the basis for unity and harmony during those difficult and disonant decades following Independence.

In any case, there is a new ethic emerging and it can be properly called a leisure-ethic. Let us now examine some of its chief elements:

"Do your own thing."

The leisure-ethic is perhaps most succinctly stated in the popular expression "do your own thing." This expression has come into our language by way of the counter-culture and may be considered a contemporary counterpart to the Puritan doctrine of calling. More important than its radical origins, however, are its radical assumptions — that each person is free and unique and that his personal dignity is not mediated through his role in any system — religious or secular.

Up to now, most Americans have been uneasy about the notion of "doing your own thing." Many of our politicians, radio evangelists, and prophets of doom have dutifully warned us of the anarchy and debauchery it supposedly invites. Such emphatic personalism has its social and psychological hazards, obviously. But so did the Protestant doctrines of Christian vocation from which the work-ethic emerged! Indeed, let us not forget that Luther's *Beruf* and Calvin's *calling* were disturbing notions in their own times and were condemned by both religious and secular authorities for their radical individualism.

From a Christian point of view, the important thing about an ethic of "doing your own thing" is not its economic and political risks, but its clear affirmation of personal dignity and freedom in the face of all the depersonalizing forces of contemporary culture — including aspects of bureaucracy, technology, and mass-media. In a time when not only science-fiction writers, but also eminent educators such as Harvard's B. F. Skinner, are suggesting that personal dignity and freedom should be sacrificed to the gods of technology and bureaucracy in order to improve our civilization's chances for salvation, a radical and virile personalism may be a healthy corrective — perhaps even our best defense against technological totalitarianism — in spite of its hazards.[2]

In any event, "doing your own thing" has become a

viable ethic — a doctrine of vocation — for increasing numbers of American young people. For some, it has meant a repudiation of the traditional systems of education and employment and a passionate quest for alternatives. For others, it has meant a more cautious selection of courses of study, more limited investments of time and energy in school and work, and more qualified commitments to institutions and organizations. For still others, it has meant the relentless and unrestrained pursuit of pleasure and self-satisfaction. Again, for others, it has meant a deeper dedication to a particular form of human service. ("Doing your own thing," you see, does not necessarily mean a repudiation of work — it often means a deeper commitment to it.)

There can be little doubt that the notion of "doing your own thing" has weakened traditional American institutions, including organized religion (and it will probably weaken them even more in the years ahead), so the concern of those charged with the preservation of these institutions is to some degree warranted. Yet, evangelical Christianity can neither escape responsibility for its historic role in promoting the values of personal dignity and freedom upon which this ethic is based nor repudiate these values at this point in time without denying the gospel itself. Instead of consuming themselves in worry and despair over the hazards of "doing your own thing," therefore, Christians should be discovering and alerting one another to its opportunities. In other words, Christians can confidently affirm this leisure-ethic as a bold expression and an audacious exercise of the freedom they have in Christ and proceed to make their "thing" the deeds of love, joy, and peace which spring forth from one whose spirit has been set free from sin and guilt!

In a time when human beings are searching for — and to some extent finding — new experiences and understandings of freedom in so many areas of their lives — and in an age when authentic freedom is so elusive — it would be tragic if the churches became so fainthearted about proclaiming the freedom which is represented by the gospel that their message comes through as rationale for repression. Unfortunately, to many young people, that often has been the case. It is no wonder, therefore, that they are "doing their own thing," including their own Jesus thing, without the ministry of the church.

"Different Strokes for Different Folks"

As a corollary to its radical affirmation of personal dignity and freedom, the leisure-ethic posits a pluralistic value system and invites a fantastic variety of acceptable life styles. There can be no personal dignity if dignity is something which is meted out to each person by his society on the basis of an external and ultimately arbitrary scheme of rewards and punishments. (This is why the so-called "dignity of work" has always been a spurious concept, because it implies that a person's dignity is somehow derived from his work and that a person who has no work has no dignity). Nor can there be genuine freedom if everyone is measured by the same scale of values or expected to follow a prescribed pattern of development and achievement. In a leisure-oriented society, people are encouraged to project widely differing goals and are offered a plethora of pathways by which to pursue them. Instead of the traditional benchmarks, such as those of educational achievement or economic success, notions like "different strokes for different folks" and "whatever turns you on, Baby" will be the basis for analyzing and evaluating human experience. As Alvin Toffler writes:

> Bizarre as some of this may sound, it would be well not to rule out the seemingly improbable, for the realm of leisure, unlike that of work, is little constrained by practical considerations. Here imagination has free play, and the mind of man can conjure up incredible varieties of "fun." Given enough time, money and, for some of these, technical skill, the men of tomorrow will be capable of playing in ways never dreamed of before.[3]

Among other things, this will revolutionize the forms and functions of our social systems, especially those of education and employment, away from patterns of conformity and processes of coercion into styles of maximum versatility and scenarios of creative change. Indeed, unless Toffler and countless other contemporary commentators who are warning us about "future shock" and our need for systems of greater adaptability are to be completely ignored, the sheer survival of the human organism in its complex and changing technological environment necessitates drastic reform of its social systems to provide greater support for human flexibility and diversity.

The very idea of a pluralistic value system and a variety of life styles is repugnant to many devout Christians. "How can something be right for some people and wrong for others?" they ask. "And how can we have any order or cooperation in our society if people are all living by different rules?" Will not pluralism ultimately result in anarchy?

These are understandable and valid fears. But two things must be kept in mind: In the first place, the complex systems on which the projections of a leisure-oriented society are based will of necessity impose certain values and patterns whether anyone likes it or not — even those who choose to repudiate bureaucracy and technology. Technological systems, for example, demand absolute rationality, absolute interdependence, absolute consistency, accuracy, and reliability or they simply do not function. A society that is based upon technological systems, therefore, will demand of its human constituents much higher levels of individual integrity and corporate cooperation than was ever required, or even hoped for, in the agrarian and early industrial stages of civilization. It is difficult to imagine how the technological systems of the future will shape human values and life styles, but it is impossible to conceive of any co-existence of technology and anarchy.

Secondly, when viewed from either a geographical or a historical perspective, the People of God have already (in fact, have almost always) experienced pluralism and diversity. From nation to nation, and from generation to generation, there have been great variations in the personal values and life styles of Christians. One needs only to consider the various Christian attitudes and practices concerning the consumption of alcohol, or service in the military, or sponsorship of education, or the roles of women, or countless other areas in which values have been involved to realize that pluralism is not some alien and subversive element in Christian experience. That which is different is that the varying systems and styles are no longer separated by time or space or both. Instead of sequential and sectional pluralism, there will emerge a simultaneous and intersecting pluralism. This will require many changes in the social institutions through which values are mediated — like re-wiring electronic sound systems for stereophonic, instead of monaural, reproductions — but the role and significance of these institutions in assisting persons to realize fulfillment of their human potential will be greatly increased. Among the institutions that will be forced to change from monaural to stereophonic systems, of course, is the church. But instead of being fearful and hesitant about all this, the church—whose life and destiny has always transcended particular times and places and whose values have repeatedly broken out of cultural captivity—should be amongst the best prepared of institutions to adapt and flourish in the world of change and variety!

Neither the rationality of technological system nor the past experience of the church will exempt contemporary Christians from great anguish and argument as pluralism and diversity spreads. Whether we like it or not, we are being compelled to choose those values and styles of life by which we shall live and to respect the right of everyone else to choose also. But instead of viewing this as a threat to Christian values, we should see this as an opportunity to purify them. Instead of sounding alarm over the abandonment of certain heretofore prescribed Christian life styles, we should welcome the opportunities to develop more authentic and imaginative ones.

"It's been good to know you"

An ethic of radical personal freedom and a pluralistic system of values will change many patterns of personal activity and relationship. For example, we can anticipate that human relationships will become more meaningful but less permanent. People will relate to one another more and more because they *want* to and less and less because they *have* to. And when they no longer want to, they will no longer relate. That hurts our notions of " 'til death do us part," but it should enable us to shorten our Christmas card lists. The challenge, of course, is to keep relationships, at least those relationships which we cherish, alive and growing (which really has been part of our mission as Christians all along!). Again, of all people in the leisure-oriented society, Christians are the best prepared, and should have the least to fear, as far as any trend towards more honesty and freedom in human relationships is concerned.

Group loyalties, as well as personal relationships,

will be put to the test. In fact, the leisure-ethic is already contributing to the decline of loyalty to one's own group or place and promoting a new cosmopolitanism. When people are free to follow their own interests, free to move from place to place, and free to circulate among various social groups, they are less inclined to identify and align themselves totally with any particular ones. In a leisure oriented society, the interests and loyalties of people are likely to be spread over a wide range of possibilities. (Ask your favorite student why he cannot get excited about Homecoming, or has so little loyalty to a particular fraternity or sorority, or fails to see any reason to join a religious club.)

This will mean, on the one hand, that people will not allow themselves to be claimed or counted upon totally by any group, including a congregation. On the other hand, it will mean that they are less apt to be caught up in the chauvinism, rivalry, and petty affairs of any particular group. Concepts of national citizenship and denominational membership may have to be revised. Hopefully, this will hasten the demise of both nationalism and denominationalism (as well as many of the other sectarian spirits that still survive and split the human family) and enable future generations to experience the full significance of concepts such as *the church* and *the world*.

"Fly Now, Pay Later" (if necessary)

One of the most significant aspects of the leisure-ethic, and undoubtedly one of its greatest hazards, is its predilection towards instant gratification at the expense of deferred rewards. Leisure man has little, if any, interest in "pie in the sky in the sweet bye and bye." He wants to live *now* — even if it means settling for Pepsi and potato chips.

Young people are already hooked on the horns of the dilemma which this aspect of the leisure-ethic represents in contemporary American society. On the one hand, they are virtually imprisoned in an educational system which is based upon the principle of deferred rewards. ("Study hard, so you can be successful when you grow up.") On the other hand, they are also being bombarded with mass-media advertising which arouses their desire for immediate satisfaction. ("Live now, pay later.") As a result of daily exposure to these conflicting channels, their psychological circuits often become jammed. Many of them have been forced to tune out both messages, preferring to risk social and economic disaster rather than suffer psychic or spiritual destruction. Others are trying desperately to articulate and help resolve the conflicts. But their parents and teachers are often too busy ("doing their own thing") to hear them.

In any case, it is apparent that the leisure revolution is generating a human species that will not wait for heavenly hospitality. If Christianity is to vie for loyalties in the leisure oriented society, it will have to offer peace and joy in the here and now as well as an ultimate hope.

"Let's get it all together"

Finally, it is apparent that an ethic of "doing your own thing" in the world of today, is not, and can never be, as individualistic a matter as it first sounds. "Doing your own thing" in the age of technology requires a supporting cast of thousands, indeed millions, of other people. Those guitars, skiis, and camping trailers were not on the agenda for the six days of creation and there are precious few forms of leisure today which can be pursued in isolation and independence from society. It was possible for men to work alone — at least as long as they worked in pastoral and agrarian economies — but men have always needed each other for play. For all its freedom, and all its diversity, and all its fluidity, a leisure-oriented society will be one which is radically interdependent.

Furthermore, the sophistication of today's technology (and tomorrow's even more so) has rendered competition between men and groups almost counterproductive. The more technology advances, the more it requires coordination and cooperation among its managers and beneficiaries. American society will learn to provide adequately for its weaker and poorer members, not because prospering Americans are getting more generous and kind but because they are beginning to realize how the well-being of others is necessary to their own. We may even learn to love our enemies, not necessarily because we are becoming any more loving as a people but because we will soon realize that we need them as markets for our goods and services.

In other words, the leisure-ethic can lead us into new discoveries and profound experiences of "brother"-hood, of "neighbor"-hood, and of community. Instead of pursuing arbitrary and elusive signs of success — which more often than not have involved invidious comparisons and envious competition between ourselves and our brother and neighbor — we can dedicate our best efforts to the enjoyment of life — which almost always involves a sharing of its gifts.

In summary, therefore, it can be said that the emerging leisure-ethic has five discernible aspects. It is based upon a radical affirmation of personal freedom, based upon the inherent dignity and uniqueness of every human being. It presupposes a pluralistic system of values and promotes a wide diversity of life styles. It compels the integrity, but dispels the permanence, of human relationships and replaces narrow group loyalties with more ecumenical attitudes and interests. It prefers immediate satisfaction over promises of future happiness. And it advances the interdependence of men and groups instead of their independence and competition.

Most Christians today will probably find it difficult to affirm all of these aspects of the leisure-ethic, but they will find it increasingly difficult to ignore or oppose them. The hazards are real, but the creative and redemptive possibilities will challenge the bravest — and freest — Christian spirits of our time. Freedom has always been a disturbing concept. It has terrified kings and popes and has threatened even the most sacred values and secure institutions.

But freedom is at the very heart of the gospel of Jesus Christ and it has been the key to the development of the Judeo-Christian tradition and modern civilization — in spite of the blindness and bungling with which it has been handled in every generation. How this generation handles the freedom which is surging in the leisure revolution, therefore, will determine the direction of both our religious tradition and the civilization it has nourished. And it is the gospel itself — not merely the fascinating and complex social changes which we are witnessing — that is calling and challenging us to new consciousness and new sharing of our freedom.

7

Toward a Style of Christian Life and Mission

As discussed in the preceding chapters, neither the decadent work-ethic nor the emerging leisure-ethic are essentially or exclusively Christian values. They have both appeared in a civilization which has been richly nourished by Christianity and they are both based upon assumptions concerning man and his relationship to God and the world which are derived from certain Christian beliefs and traditions. But in both cases, the chief dynamic of their development has been economic, rather than religious, and their relationship to Christian teaching and practice has been a selective and self-serving one.

This work-ethic, for example, received its religious credentials, not from Jesus Christ and the New Testament church, but from the theology of John Calvin and the tradition of the Puritans. Calvinism's emphasis upon the absolute sovereignty of God and total depravity of man provided the theological foundations for a life style of austerity and for concepts of morality that exaggerated the personal commitment, responsibility, and discipline of Christians at the expense of their freedom and joy as living and loving creatures.

The time has now come to endow the leisure-ethic with a similar set of operative religious credentials. There are as many resources in Scripture and in Christian tradition to validate and energize a leisure-ethic as there have been to support a work-ethic. One of the central tasks of today's theologians is to identify these resources and relate them to the contemporary, post-industrial milieu, just as the Reformation theologians did for the post-medieval milieu. Without these resources, Christians will flounder pitifully themselves and miss their great opportunities for mission in the leisure-oriented society.

What are some of these resources? What are the elements that constitute a Christian life style in a leisure-oriented society? How does a person relate his faith and hope as a Christian to his life of leisure?

In the second chapter, we suggested that Christians should re-examine their notions about work, play and worship and re-arrange the relationships into which they have been forced by the prevailing mores of modern middle-class society. In Chapter 5, we offered some new definitions of leisure with which to replace false and misleading ones. In Chapter 6, we described the emerging leisure-ethic and spelled out some of its implications for Christians. Now it is time to offer some specific concepts around which a distinctive and authentic Christian life style can be developed.

I. The ABC's of Christian Life Style in a Leisure-oriented Society

As a beginning, let us consider three simple concepts — abandon, beauty, and celebration. Properly understood, these concepts will offer some creative possibilities for the revitalization of personal faith and will provide the church with an approach to leisure which is both theologically appropriate and culturally relevant.

Abandon

Along with their experience of Christian *commitment,* today's Christians need a concept of *abandon.* Abandon means to leave behind, to move away from, to forsake, or simply to let go. A concept of Christian abandon means to LET GOD!

The early Christians paid little attention to the affairs of this world. They were filled with anticipation of the return of Christ and the establishment of a heavenly kingdom. Spiritual activity superseded their interest in worldly work.

Since the Reformation, the pendulum has swung the other way. Christians have taken upon themselves the burdens of this world and set themselves to the task of establishing the kingdom of God. In fact, many Christians have become so involved in saving the world from this scourge or that calamity, that they seem to have lost their trust in the power and promises of God. As a result, their Christian commitment leads them into frustration and despair over the failure of their efforts to solve the problems of the world and establish a perfect society.

Furthermore, many Christians, indeed many congregations and denominations, are simply carrying too much of their own accumulated baggage. They cling to memories and mementos of the past as if they had some eternal value while they squander the priceless moments of insight and opportunity that come with each new day. Instead of running with Jesus in the life of today, they are still looking for him in the tombs of yesterday.

Men cannot experience leisure until they learn to travel light.

Abandon means to take seriously Jesus' counsel to "Be not anxious about your life" and to accept Luther's admonition to live boldly in the forgiveness of sin. It means to trust radically in the love and wisdom of God as far as one's own life is concerned — and as far as the world is concerned.

Christian commitment is still very important, but it needs to be stripped of its perfectionism and presumption. No Christian can bear the burdens of another, or of society, unless he is able and willing to cast his own burdens upon Christ. (Is that a new idea?) This means that the more complex and problematical modern life becomes, the more Christians will need a concept of *abandon* to enable them to disentangle and disengage themselves from its cares and confusion.

It is perhaps time to rip out of our hymnbooks some of those classic Calvinist hymns like "Work, for the Night Is Coming" and "Onward Christian Soldiers" and replace them with some less strenuous and presumptuous songs like the Beatles' "Let It Be" or Ocean's "Put Your Hand in the Hand of the Man from Galilee." We need to be reminded that our hope is in the work of God, not in our own striving for improvement.

The responsibilities of Christians will not be lessened in a leisure-oriented society, but without authentic experiences and understandings of Christian freedom, these responsibilities will become brutal and depressing. To live freely and joyfully in an age of profound anxiety, to find meaning in a world of enormous complexity, and to avoid being reduced to mere components in their technological systems, Christians need a concept of freedom which is more radical than ever before. The gospel must free modern man, not only from the tyranny of sin, death, and the power of the devil, but also from the tyranny of their worldly commitments — including even those of family and friends — and enable them to experience fully the ecstasy of freedom and grace. In other words, Christian freedom today must have an element of *abandon* or it will be a false and elusive freedom.

Beauty

Christian life style in a leisure-oriented society will include a dramatic realignment of the relationships between beauty and necessity. For centuries the medieval church exalted aesthetic considerations above utilitarian ones in its affirmation of the arts, its development of universities, its construction of cathedrals, and its emphasis upon worship. The rationalizing and secularizing forces which were set into motion by the Renaissance and the Reformation, however, have progressively advanced functional and practical considerations, often at the expense (although not necessarily so) of aesthetic and spiritual values. Today, nearly all of nature, art, man, and society have been thoroughly analyzed, computed, and reduced to quantitative and componential values. Human beings have been broken down into a network of organs and processes. Human life has been reduced to roles and functions.

Modern man, *homo faber,* the manipulator and manager of the creation, has a highly developed sense of survival and control, but he has all but lost his sense of awe and wonder. His desire to conquer and discover has eroded his capacity for appreciation and reverence.

Immanuel Kant once wrote that man's sin is greatest when he enjoys that which is intended to be used and when he uses that which is to be enjoyed. The work-ethic has inspired a morality of use; the leisure-ethic will inspire a morality of enjoyment.

But in order to enjoy life, men must have a sense of *beauty.* They must be able to see and feel beauty in themselves, in each other, and in their environment — including their technological environment. In times of scarcity, beauty was often sacrificed in the interest of utility, but the material and cultural wealth that has unleashed a leisure revolution offers countless opportunities for aesthetic as well as economic abundance.

When Jesus said "I came that they may have life, and have it abundantly," he was promising much more than the satisfaction of physical and social needs. He came offering men a quality and style of life that went far beyond comfort and convenience. In fact, he called men away from the pursuit of these mundane interests and pointed them toward a fuller, more wonderful, more exciting, more beautiful experience of human life.[1]

Today's leisure man needs a sense of beauty to enable him to use his freedom creatively and responsibly. Without it, his liberation will become license and his freedom will deteriorate into exploitation and obscenity. The leisure revolution offers Christianity its greatest opportunities since the Middle Ages to provide its culture with aesthetic and spiritual nourishment. Unless Christians themselves have a passion for beauty, however, those opportunities will slip by unnoticed.

> Men are so inclined to content themselves with what is commonplace; the spirit and the senses so easily grow dead to the impressions of the beautiful and perfect, that everyone should study, by all methods, to nourish in his mind the faculty of feeling these things. For no man can bear to be entirely deprived of such enjoyment.[2]

Celebration

To refresh and fortify their discipleship, contemporary Christians need rich experiences of *celebration*.

Today's Christians are already doing their fair share of complaining about the miseries of the world, but they are often failing to celebrate its joys and mysteries. Their agendas are so crowded with evils to be attacked, problems to be solved, and needs to be met, that they have no time or energy for praise and thanksgiving for all their blessings. Even the calendar of the church, which is based upon the traditional feasts and festivals of the liturgical year, has become so cluttered with causes that the celebrative character of worship becomes smothered and soured by social concern.

It has been often said that the greatest argument against Christianity is the unhappy expression most Christians wear on their faces. Look around you the next time your congregation *celebrates* (???) the Eucharist!

Unfortunately, too many Christians are suspicious of any form of celebration. Celebration suggests immoderate behavior and at least hints at immorality. Some avoid celebration because it may entail a waste of time, or money, or energy — an appropriate attitude for times of scarcity, perhaps, but hardly justifiable for most Christians in America today. (Furthermore, it has often been the peoples who were most poor and insecure who were the most ready for celebration.) Others have feared celebration because it promotes emotional expression and exposes people to one another in unguarded ways — but what could be more appropriate for those who are seeking to fill the world with love, joy, and peace?

To celebrate means to emphasize, to highlight, to

translate the ordinary into the extraordinary. When we celebrate, we raise the power of certain events, circumstances, or relationships to their highest power and transform them into moments of great affirmation and ecstasy. To celebrate is to respond to the gift of life with a loud "Yes!"

There are hazards in celebration, to be sure, but when a Christian celebrates, he is praising God from whom all blessings flow.

Much more could be written about each of these concepts — *abandon, beauty,* and *celebration* — but our purpose in these pages is merely to suggest some beginnings. With these concepts as the ABC's, however, almost any Christian can go on to develop a leisure vocabulary which can be validated theologically as well as psychologically in his daily life.

II. Ministry in a Leisure-oriented Society

The classic modalities of Christian ministry — the prophetic, the priestly, and the kingly — provide an excellent conceptual framework for the consideration of ministry and mission in a leisure-oriented society. Together with an expanded concept of pastoral functions, these modalities will give both focus and force to whatever type of leisure ministry is undertaken.

A. The Prophetic Ministry

The prophetic task in leisure ministry will be that of exposing the inequities and exploitation of our economic and social systems. Above all, it will be concerned with what Alexis de Tocqueville once called the "virtuous materialism" of American democratic society.

More than 100 years ago, Tocqueville noted that the influence of Puritan morality upon their economic and social patterns would probably prevent Americans from falling prey to the gross sins and forbidden pleasures that had so often corrupted European aristocracies. But he also observed that Americans were inclined to let themselves become absorbed and enervated by pleasures which are permitted — especially those which suggest achievement and success. A "virtuous material-ism" therefore prevails among Americans.[3] Writing a half-century later, Thorstein Veblen savagely attacked this materialism, suggesting that its "virtue" exists only in the minds of those who indulge themselves in it.[4]

There is indeed a prophetic ministry to be taken up in a society that allows two million families to have second homes when there are still several million other families who are homeless. There is a message from God to be delivered to a people which spends more on its household pets than it does on its dependent senior citizens. There is a word from the Lord for a nation that spends more to kill each Vietnamese than to edu-cate each American, a government that is more willing to guarantee fair profits for some of its powerful cor-porations than full stomachs for some of its powerless people.

It will take prophetic ministry to get American society away from its orgy of production and consump-tion. In terms of materialistic values, our economic system is working well — we are producing and consuming at an accelerating rate with no small credit due to our popular notions about work and leisure.

Ironically, the system which is rewarding us for our work so splendidly in materialistic terms is actually penalizing us in spiritual and cultural terms. It dictates that everyone must organize his life around his work and offers material rewards for competence and diligence. Actually, however, those who work best are often singled out for special punishment by being promoted to positions that demand more work. If a man commits himself wholeheartedly to his career, the chances are good that he will be penalized (i.e., "promoted") again and again until his whole life gets absorbed into his work and he has neither the time nor the energy for anything else — until he is saved by a heart attack or liberated by compulsory retirement.

To make matters worse, each of those so-called promotions a worker receives carries with it the additional curse of a salary increase and an advance in social status. That usually means that he has to raise his standard of living, i.e., consume more material goods. Whatever time and energy he has left after working, therefore, goes into consuming. Some people are trying to call that leisure. They must be exposed and exorcised! There is, indeed, a need for prophetic ministry.

B. *The Priestly Ministry*

The priestly task in leisure ministry is that of providing the opportunities for true celebration. Perhaps more than ever before, men and women need to have their spirits lifted above their crowded agendas and busy schedules. They need opportunities to become totally, even if temporarily, disengaged from the concerns of their work and play in the world and catch glimpses of transcendent realities.

It is wonderful to be able to be free of economic and social constraint, but that is not enough. Men need to be spiritually, psychologically, and emotionally released as well. Western Christianity has traditionally focused its priestly ministry upon man's sin and guilt, but priestly ministry must also address itself to the creative and dynamic potential with which every man has been endowed. It is not enough to keep beating down the Old Adam, ministry must encourage the New Man in Christ!

The freedom that leisure offers will be shallow and slippery unless there are occasions when it is nourished and stimulated by extravagant, even ecstatic experience. Unless men have opportunities to embrace one another in cultic and mythic solidarity, their freedom will become an alienating and atomizing factor and their relationships will atrophy into mere functional attachments.

In the face of a leisure society's need for creative forms of celebration, however, it is distressing that so many so-called leisure ministries have settled for little more than clever ways of merchandising superficial religious experience. Except for a sense of novelty and perhaps some more impressive statistics, for example, there is little gained by taking over a drive-in movie theater for a Sunday morning worship service. Nor does hanging a set of loudspeakers in a camp-ground or dispensing bread and wine at the end of a ski run constitute any real celebration. These strategies usually offer merely the forms of Christian celebration without its substance and further contribute to the symptoms of atomization which are already abundant in most leisure communities and situations.

In contrast to Buddhism, Hinduism and several other world religions, Christianity has a tremendous investment in the tradition of regularly gathering families and friends together to re-affirm their loyalty to Christ and their solidarity with one another. It would be unfortunate if that investment were to be squandered away with gimmicks that promise, but do not deliver, the experience of celebration which are required by and relevant to a leisure-oriented society.

In any event, whether it happens at the drag strip, in the shopping center, in the stadium parking lot, or in the quaint old building on the corner across from the gas station, there will be a priestly ministry to conduct and it will probably become both more crucial and more creative than ever before.

C. *The Kingly Ministry*

The most crucial ministry of all, however, may be the kingly one. In fact, without it there may not ever be a leisure-oriented society. Instead, we might see Aldous Huxley's *Brave New World* or George Orwell's

1984. Technology must be made to serve men, or men will become the slaves of technology. We have already discussed the production-consumption spiral which manipulates human values and appetites to stimulate the flow of money and goods.

An even larger issue is to what extent American society will continue to allow its military-industrial complex to dominate the development and direction of its technology. Who will decide whether our technology will be used to help destroy or enjoy life upon earth? Who determines whether the time, talents and treasures of men shall be committed to destructive and frivolous things or things that will enhance the quality of life?

A society oriented around an ethic of "doing your own thing" will need a complex system of law and order. Pluralistic value systems will have to be somehow harmonized and there must be an orchestration of life styles if anarchy and chaos are to be averted. The issues of authority and the distribution of power will become fantastically sophisticated. Without a kingly ministry, rooted in the heritage from which we have come but responsive to the new circumstances in which we find ourselves, our super-sophisticated systems may simply self-destruct. In fact, there are some signs indicating that we had better not wait much longer and some people saying that it is already too late. Kingly ministry, addressed to the issues of authority and control in an age of technology has never before been so vitally needed, nor so feebly offered.

D. *The Roles of Clergy and Laymen*

In suggesting the basic elements of Christian life style and describing the modalities of ministry in a leisure-oriented society, distinctions between clergy and laity have been deliberately avoided. In other words, the paragraphs above apply to both pastors and laymen. For a variety of reasons, the leisure revolution will translate the doctrine of the universal priesthood of all believers from what has often been a pious fiction into a functional reality. On the one hand, no single type of religious professional will be able to develop the competence required to perform, or direct, or even coordinate all of the varieties of ministry which will be called for in the complex and ever-changing leisure society. On the other hand, there will be new opportunities for leadership and special service by nearly everyone. In fact, it is quite possible that the distinction between clergy and laity will virtually disappear.

In any case, the role and function of religious professionals will continue the trend from the more authoritative to the more facilitative. The pastor will probably be doing less and less preaching, teaching, and supervising. Instead, he will be moving more and more among individuals, turning them on to new interests and ideas, bringing them together on the basis of common concerns, and plugging them into the systems where they can get whatever they need or contribute whatever they have to offer. In simple terms, the pastor will be a facilitator — a facilitator of freedom, of celebration, of poignancy and quality of life.

The professional minister's role in a technological society is already ambiguous and marginal. The shift from authoritative to facilitative functions may appear to make it more so, but in reality both the office and the person will benefit. There will be less pious mystique and less compulsive diligence. Above all, there will be emancipation from the haunting feeling of being privately judged by their constituencies as third-rate entertainers, mediocre educators, or cheap psychiatrists. Who knows, the pastor of tomorrow may even dare to be leisurely?

The most significant developments in ministry, however, will be related to the new challenge and opportunities which leisure presents to laymen. The more people are able to limit their investment of time and energy in work that is necessary, i.e., their jobs, the more freely they will be able to invest themselves in voluntary service — at home and abroad. Laymen with special interests and skills will find countless new opportunities to utilize and develop them without having to be so concerned about their monetary value. Instead of using their talents only for self gain, they can dedicate them to God as an offering of themselves in response to his love and blessing.

The worship of work and the emphasis upon competitive processes have built our great economic and social empires, but they have robbed us of much of the joy and freedom which accompanies authentic service to one's neighbor. In our systems, service is regarded as another commodity to be bought and sold. This has often meant that we withhold our service from those who cannot pay or, if we do offer it without expectation of compensation, that it becomes patronizing and manipulative. The leisure revolution is changing that. Many young people, at least, are more ready to offer themselves in ministry to the needs of others than they are to commit themselves to educational and employment programs that will guarantee them affluence and prestige. A new spirit of voluntarism is one of the keys to ministry in a leisure oriented society — and it is a key that is in the hands of the laity, rather than the clergy.

8

Work, Play, and Worship —Getting It All Together

At the beginning of this book, we identified work, play and worship as the general components of Christian life style in contemporary American society. We suggested, however, that because our society has so exalted the value of work, all three of these elements have become distorted in the experience of most Christians today and have led many into patterns of despair and self-destruction. We have attempted to show how a leisure revolution is forcing us to re-examine our notions about work, play and worship and suggested that a proper understanding of leisure can help us correct the distortion and liberate us for more abundant life and more relevant mission in the emerging leisure-oriented society.

There is much at stake here, whether measured in terms of the drastic changes in personal values and life-styles which can be anticipated or in terms of the massive shifts in social institutions and processes which are forthcoming. It may be presumptuous to call it a "new reformation," but it would be tragically short-sighted to dismiss the leisure trends as mere fads and phases from which some sort of return to normalcy will soon emerge. We have seen an abundance of leisure fads, to be sure, and we shall undoubtedly see more, but we are concerned here with the longer trends. Unless we dismantle our technological para-dise—or blow it to bits—we are not likely, for example, to see increases in the average American's work-week or work-life. Nor are there any plans to build airplanes that fly more slowly or computers that perform less efficiently.

There is no return to the past, but there are alterna-tive futures. Work, play and worship have taken dif-ferent forms for different generations and we can ex-pect to see even greater variations and more rapid changes in times to come. The crucial task for Chris-tians will be to establish appropriate relationships and priorities among them in order to facilitate authentic experiences of fulfillment and transcendence.

Work will continue to be necessary and good. For the vast majority of Americans, at least, and for the rest of mankind, it will continue to be the chief basis for obtaining a livelihood and for contributing to the com-mon weal. But work will not be worshiped and glorified. It will be clearly seen as a means, not an end. It may confer upon men their standard of material prosperity, but not their human dignity and freedom.

Work systems, i.e., industries, bureaucracies, etc., will continue to flourish, but they will not be allowed to dictate the personal habits, values, and calendars of their participants. Indeed, the participants will reshape the work systems to accommodate their other interests—including those of play and worship. As the German sociologist, Dietrich von Oppen, has pointed out, the systems of the post-industrial age, while complex and powerful, have nevertheless been stripped of their sacrosanct and tyrannizing values. In contrast to medieval and early industrial institutions, the contemporary and emergent ones are flexible and adaptable in the face of changing human demands.

> No method of work, no demarcation of authority, no chain of command, and no form of cooperation is sacred and inviolable. Employment . . . is settled simply by contract or written statement, and no longer with the oath or pledge. . . .[1]

Furthermore, the success of modern work systems is directly related, not to their authority and immutability, but to the freedom and creativity which they allow and promote among the persons who people them. Neither loyalty nor productivity can be coerced; they must come as the result of free choice by the workers— or not at all. It follows, therefore, that it is in the interest of the work systems themselves to accentuate and extend the freedom and dignity of all who participate in them.

Ironically, as our idolatry of work is dispelled, it will take on greater, not lesser, meaning in our total life style because it will be a liberating, rather than an inhibiting, factor. As work is divested of its compulsive and coercive aspects, it becomes more easily integrated with play. For those who are truly liberated, i.e. those who are free in spirit, work actually becomes play.

For most people, however, work presents too narrow a range of opportunities for the full expression of their freedom and dignity. It would be nice if everyone could get paid for doing their own thing, but our technological and bureaucratic systems are not likely to be that accommodating. We will need regular occasions for play, therefore, in order to expand our creativity and self-expression, to experience fantasy and festivity, to share ecstasy and wonder.

Having discovered the educational, therapeutic and reconciling aspects of play, as well as acknowledged the role of play in scientific and technological over-leaps, it is highly doubtful that we will ever again attempt to repress play in the name of morality and religion or in the interests of economic growth. A greater danger, perhaps, is that the generation which has shattered the idols of work will be tempted to bow down before the gods of play—sacrificing their new freedom and dignity upon the altars of pleasure in liturgies of distraction and frivolous pursuits. As one of the professors at Minnesota, Arthur L. Johnson, tells his sociology class, "It sometimes appears that Americans are enjoying the highest standard of low living in history."

The challenge to contemporary American Christians, therefore, is to find ways of affirming both work and play without becoming absorbed in either or both of them. The only way to do that, of course, is to place them both in a broader context of life's meaning and purpose — and subject them to the discipline of a higher authority. In other words, work and play should be experienced and understood, not as separate and, in a sense, antithetical elements, but as the dynamic interfacing of our responses to a gracious and caring God. The key to a Christian understanding of work and play, therefore, lies in worship.

Worship in this sense, however, means much more than scheduled occasions for pious noises and sentimental recollections—whether as part of a traditional congregation or at the drive-in theater on the way to the lake. The worship that God expects—and that leisure inspires—involves a continuous response of gladness and hope through every experience of life—including its work and play—and a daily discipline of service and self-examination in the context of the Law's claim upon us and the gospel's call to freedom and maturity. (It may even be better if some of our scheduled religious exercises were cancelled and Christians were more often encouraged to "do their own thing" in celebration of their faith, hope and love.)

Some exciting things are happening in our experience and understanding of worship today—on our campuses, at our retreat centers, and even in many homes and congregations. Like work and play, worship is taking new forms and new meanings. It is the leisure revolution which is propelling many of these changes—and it is through a new appreciation of leisure that we shall experience the redemptive relationships between work, play and worship.

Our inherited, work-valued social and economic systems have conditioned us to worship our work, to work at our play, and to play at our worship. If we are bold enough to meet the challenges of the leisure revolution and begin laying the spiritual, as well as the institutional, foundations for a leisure-oriented society, we will find it increasingly possible to experience our work as play, to see our play as worship, and to make worship our work. That will not consumate the kingdom of heaven, but it will certainly enable the body of Christ to raise its life and mission in this world to new heights of ecstasy.

Notes

Chapter 1

1. Everyone who writes about work, play or worship has his own definitions of these terms. The works cited in the bibliography contain many such definitions and they are all in some sense relevant. The concern of this book, however, will be for integrating these concepts into an adequate definition of leisure.

Chapter 2

1. Walter Kerr, *The Decline of Pleasure,* p. 39

2. Romans 12:1.

3. Arnold Toynbee, writing in the *London Observer,* July, 1971

Chapter 3

1. The New York Electrical Workers Union — established a 25-hour work week as early as 1966.

2. Riva Poor, *4 Days, 40 Hours, Reporting on a Revolution in Work and Leisure*, Also *Poor's Workweek Letter*, Vol. 1. No. 1, (July 1, 1971)

3. *Minneapolis Star*, July 1, 1971

4. *Playboy*, October, 1971, p. 21

5. *Changing Times*, June, 1971, p. 36

6. These statistics on education and retirement are taken from Census Bureau data and projections.

7. *Changing Times*, June, 1971, p. 35

8. Herman Kahn and Anthony J. Wiener, *The Year Two Thousand*.

9. "Leisure: Investment Opportunities in a 150 Billion Dollar Market," Merrill Lynch, Pierce, Fenner, and Smith, Incorporated, p. 2

10. *Changing Times*, June, 1971, p. 37

11. "Leisure: Investment Opportunities, etc." pp. 3-4

12. *Changing Times*, June 1971, p. 36

13. As reported by the National Industrial Recreation Association

14. "Leisure: Investment Opportunities, etc." pp. 3-4

15. *Changing Times*, June 1971, p. 37

16. From a 1970 study of state travel development by the Discover America Travel Organization, Washington, D.C.

17. Theodore Levitt, *Harvard Business Review*

18. For an interpretation of the younger generation's revolt against technocratic society, read Theodore Roszak's *The Making of a Counter Culture*.

19. Charles A. Reich, *The Greening of America*, pp. 4-5

20. Ian H. Wilson, "The New Reformation," *The Futurist*, Vol. V., No. 3 (June, 1971) p. 105

Chapter 4

1. Karl Marx (1818-1883), German political philosopher and one of the founders of the German Social Democratic Labor Party. His famous work *Das Kapital* was published in three volumes, beginning in 1867 and completed by Friedrich Engels in 1895.

   Alexis de Tocqueville (1805-1859), French nobleman, diplomat, and historian. His famous work *Democratic en Amérique (Democracy in America)* was published in two volumes in 1835 and 1839.

   Max Weber (1864-1920), German historian and sociologist. His famous work *Die Protestantische Ethik und der Geist des Kapitalismus (The Protestant Ethic and the Spirit of Capitalism)* was first published in Germany in 1904 and translated to English by Talcott Parsons in 1930.

2. Genesis 3:17-24

3. Exodus 20:8-11; Deuteronomy 5:12-14; Leviticus 23:1-8, 15-21, 26-32, 33-36. (Note the repeated emphasis upon the prohibition of work.)

4. For example, see the parable of the rich young ruler (Matthew 19:16-30; Mark 10:17-31; Luke 18:18-30) and the parable of the great banquet (Matthew 22:1-10; Luke 14:15-24)

5. Sebastian de Grazia, *Of Time, Work and Leisure,* pp. 23-24.

6. Weber, p. 207.

7. Tocqueville, Book II, p. 319.

8. *Ibid*. p. 160.

9. Richard M. Nixon, Labor Day Message, September 6, 1971.

10. De Grazia, "Leisure — The Broader View" (An address presented to a conference on leisure sponsored by the University of Minnesota, the Minnesota Council of Churches, and Leisure Studies, Incorporated, at St. Paul, Minnesota, February 9, 1970.

11. *Ibid*.

Chapter 5

1. For a revealing historical treatment of the understanding of man as "worker" and "player," read Johan Huizinga's *Homo Ludens: A Study of the Play Element in Culture.*

2. Oliver Wendell Holmes Jr., Memorial Day Address, Cambridge, Massachusetts, 1884.

3. Unless one projects some drastic interruption in the course of world history, such as a nuclear war that obliterates mankind or destroys American civilization, the only alternative to a leisure-oriented society is a totalitarian system based upon centralized control of sophisticated technology, such as that prophecied by George Orwell in *1984.*

Chapter 6

1. The "new consciousness" is discussed by Charles Reich in *The Greening of America.* John C. Cooper describes the same phenomenon as *The New Mentality.* Ian H. Wilson, writing in *The Futurist* (June, 1971) says that the social changes which are implied constitute "The New Reformation."

2. B. F. Skinner, *Beyond Freedom and Dignity.*

3. Alvin Toffler, *Future Shock,* p. 256-257.

Chapter 7

1. John 10:10.

2. From *Wilhelm Meister's Apprenticeship,* Johann Wolfgang von Goethe, (1799-1832).

3. Alexis de Tocqueville, *Democracy in America,* Vol. II, p. 145F.

4. Thorstein Veblen, *The Theory of the Leisure Class.*

Chapter 8

1. Dietrich von Oppen, *The Age of the Person,* p. 44.

Bibliography

Braden, William, *The Age of Aquarius,* Quadrangle Books, Chicago, 1970.

Brightbill, Charles K., *The Challenge of Leisure,* Prentice-Hall, Inc., Englewood Cliffs, N.J., 1960.

Cox, Harvey, *The Feast of Fools,* Harvard University Press, Cambridge, 1969.

de Grazia, Sebastian, *Of Time, Work, and Leisure,* Doubleday and Company, Garden City, N.Y., 1962.

de Tocqueville, Alexis, *Democracy in America,* Alfred A. Knopf, New York, 1954.

Friedmann, Georges, *The Anatomy of Work, Labor, Leisure, and the Implications of Automation,* Glencoe Free Press, New York, 1961.

Huizinga, Johan, *Homo Ludens: A Study of the Play Element in Culture,* Beacon Press, Boston, 1950.

Kahn, Herman and Anthony Wiener, *The Year 2000, A Framework for Speculation on the Next Thirty-three Years,* Mac-Millan, New York, 1967.

Kaplan, Max, *Technology, Human Values, and Leisure,* Abingdon, Nashville, 1971.

Kerr, Walter, *The Decline of Pleasure,* Simon and Schuster, New York, 1965.

Lee, Robert, *Religion and Leisure in America,* Abingdon Press, New York, 1964.

Linder, Steffan B., *The Harried Leisure Class,* Columbia University Press, New York, 1970.

Neale, Robert E., *In Praise of Play,* Harper and Row, New York, 1969.

Pieper, Josef, *Leisure, The Basis of Culture,* New American Library, New York, 1952.

Poor, Riva (ed.), *4 Days, 40 Hours, Reporting a Revolution in Work and Leisure,* Bursk and Poor Publishing, Cambridge, Mass., 1970.

Potter, David M., *People of Plenty, Economic Abundance and the American Character,* University of Chicago Press, Chicago, 1954.

Rahner, Hugo, *Man at Play,* Herder and Herder, New York, 1967.

Reich, Charles A., *The Greening of America,* Random House, New York, 1970.

Revel, Jean-Francois, *Without Marx or Jesus,* Doubleday, New York, 1971.

Riesman, David, *Abundance for What?, and Other Essays,* Doubleday Anchor Books, New York.

Roszak, Theodore, *The Making of a Counter Culture,* Doubleday and Company, Garden City, N.Y., 1969.

Theobald, Robert, *The Challenge of Abundance,* New American Library, New York, 1961.

Toffler, Alvin, *Future Shock,* Random House, New York, 1970.

von Oppen, Dietrich, *The Age of the Person,* Fortress Press, Philadelphia, 1969.

Weber, Max, *The Protestant Ethic and the Spirit of Capitalism,* Charles Scribner's Sons, New York, (first published in German in 1904-05), 1958.

Wheeler, Harvey, *Democracy in a Revolutionary Era,* Center for the Study of Democratic Institutions, Santa Barbara, Calif., 1970.

Winter, Gibson, *Being Free, Reflections on America's Cultural Revolution,* Macmillan, New York, 1970.

WORK, PLAY, AND WORSHIP

IN A LEISURE-ORIENTED SOCIETY

WORK, PLAY, AND WORSHIP STUDY GUIDE

by James B. Olson

© 1972 Augsburg Publishing House
Minneapolis, Minnesota 55415

About the Guide and Its Use

Although this study guide addresses groups, an individual can easily adapt its suggestions to independent study.

The individual will find this guide helpful in (1) identifying what to look for when reading the book, or (2) providing a way of wrapping up what has been read.

The group desiring to study *Work, Play, and Worship* may be (1) an existing group interested in studying an issue, (2) a group convened specifically to study this book, or (3) a group resulting from mutual interest generated by individuals having read the book.

The subject under consideration is appropriate for groups of adult couples and singles, senior high teens, and young adults.

Regardless of group size or meeting conditions, someone within the group must act as discussion starter, referee, gadfly, or devil's advocate. The task of leadership may be shared or rotated in the group rather than carried by one person throughout the study. The aim of the leader should be constant, however,

* to listen to the group's reactions and interpretations of the author's thought,
* to clarify and/or summarize,
* to make sure the members take seriously the author's arguments while expressing their own opinions and reactions.

In planning for a group to use this book and guide, a leader should be designated for the first meeting. That person should have read the entire book and be prepared to introduce it in an enthusiastic way, stimulating interest and curiosity. The leader should also plan to introduce the people to one another so that they will feel comfortable in the group. (Look at suggestion 1 for the first session and suggestion 2 for the second meeting. Even introductions can relate to the content of this study!) It should be the understanding of everyone (and said at times) that participants will read the chapters and be prepared to discuss the author's points as well as their own ideas.

Consider this guide as suggestive. Select questions and ideas that promote reflection and raise issues vital to your

group. Discard the study guide if your own procedure frees
you more in your study. Create an open atmosphere for everyone. Be leisurely! (Perhaps you will need to discover the
content of the word, *leisure*. At this point it is simply an
admonition to avoid the pressures of "We've got to cover
eight more pages yet today," and "But we've got to cover the
whole book!" Leisure is a challenge to pleasurable encounter
of ideas and persons.)

Let us play!

Additional copies are available from Augsburg Publishing
House: 10¢ each, $1.10 per dozen.

Preface

"Most contemporary Americans--including those who consider themselves as and struggle to be Christians--experience life as fragments of work, fragments of play, and fragments of worship. There are all too few experiences of their harmony and wholeness" (pp. 8-9). From that observation author Gordon Dahl begins his study of the role of work and play in contemporary society.

The book is addressed to young, middle-class American Christians. It provides theological reflection on work and play (whose pursuit dominates their lives)--issues which have primarily been considered in economic and social terms. *Work, Play, and Worship* describes how we are all caught up in a "leisure revolution." It presents insights and interpretation which assist in understanding the possibilities and problems of work and play today. It offers resources for creating a life-style that affirms leisure as a life-giving value enriching both work and worship.

The author is campus pastor at the University of Minnesota and a founder/director of Leisure Studies, Inc. (a leisure education organization). The book is an outgrowth of his professional and academic experiences and his concern for understanding the roles of work, play, and worship in their theological, ethical, economic, and social contexts. He writes to stimulate inquiry and to initiate discussion; those who want full or final answers to the issues involved in this study will not find them.

The ideas encountered will stimulate reflection, perhaps even provoke controversy. It is hoped that the readers will grow in their understanding, reflection, evaluation, and sharing of themselves and their involvement in the life of our world as they work, play, and worship. If this is achieved-- even in small measure--then work, play, and worship all can offer the key to survival and renewal in the 70s.

Our Present Attitudes and Understanding of Leisure
Chapter 1

A first goal should be to identify opinions people now hold toward work and leisure and to begin reflecting on the role of work and leisure in our society today.

Suggested procedure:

1. Ask members of the group to introduce themselves by briefly telling something about themselves. Make note of these introductory comments and put them aside for reference at the next meeting.

2. Distribute a copy of *Work, Play, and Worship* to each couple or person. Ask the group to read Chapters 2 and 3, pages 11-40, for the next time. They should jot down comments and questions, mark statements they endorse or dispute. Remind the participants to be alert to attitudes toward work and play exhibited in the public media.

3. Read the preface (pp. 5-6) to become acquainted with the author's viewpoint and concern. Also check out the author's objectives (in the last three paragraphs of Chapter 1) for writing the book.

4. React to the terms *work, play,* and *worship*. List these words on chart paper or on the blackboard. Reflect on what your definitions or associations reveal about your present understanding and attitude toward work and leisure. Then read the first three paragraphs of Chapter 1 and compare your reflections with the author's introductory description of our idea of work, play, and worship.

5. Reflect on why a study of leisure is important for Christians today. In its reflection of the book, does the group express areas of concern, understanding, or values which the study focuses on?

In the Midst of Revolution
Chapters 2-3

Identify the main themes. Give consideration to the roles of work, play, and worship in our society; and survey the trends which profile the "leisure revolution."

Questions for discussion or further thought:

1. The statement "Most middle-class Americans tend to worship their work, to work at their play, and to play at their worship" (p. 12) describes the confusion about their roles in our lives. What agreement, or disagreement, does this statement bring out in the group? From what does the confusion arise? What values or attitudes have contributed to the problem?

2. On page 13 the author contends that work defines our identity in our society and shapes the direction and dynamics of our lives. Did the introductions at the group's last meeting illustrate how work gives us identity? How does work become destructive (idolatrous)? On what grounds does the author criticize popular moral and religious attitudes toward work?

3. What are the implications of the thesis that many Americans simply don't know how to play?

4. How does violence affect our attitude toward play? Refer to pages 17-18. Is there a relationship between violence and the phenomenal growth of spectator sports?

5. Do you agree or disagree with the critique of American worship life? Why have churches' responses to these problems been superficial?

6. Survey the 10 social and economic trends described in Chapter 3. It would be helpful if they were listed on the blackboard or charted in view of the group. Which trends have you experienced directly? How is your life-style affected by these trends? Are they negative or positive influences? Which of the trends will have significant impact on your community in the near future? How are other individuals or groups in the community (minority groups, the unemployed, the aged, the countercultures, etc.) affected by these trends?

7. The growth of leisure in modern American society has paralleled economic and industrial growth. How has leisure been

affected by this growth? What does a consumptive leisure-ethic result in?

8. How does change in the size and shape of the work week affect leisure? If the participants have experienced a four-day work week, or are familiar with reports of these experiments, it would be interesting to have them tell the group of their experience. How do employees view work in this situation? How are life-styles affected? What attitudes develop toward leisure?

9. Why couldn't many of these trends have happened without governmental participation? In what areas has government been primarily involved?

10. How would you summarize what the "leisure revolution" is?

Work and Leisure
Chapters 4-5

Identify the main themes. Discuss the religious attitudes and economic development which contributed to the emergence of the work-ethic and created difficulty in understanding leisure.

Questions for discussion or further thought:

1. Trace the historical development of our attitude toward work through biblical times, medieval Catholicism, the Reformation, and the Puritan era. What elements have contributed to the American work-ethic? Which has made the deepest impact on the formation of the work-ethic?

2. Why do three 19th-century Europeans--Marx, Weber, and Tocqueville--have such influence on our understanding of 20th-century American religion and economics?

3. Why did Luther replace the concept of *vocatio* with the concept of *Beruf*? How did this affect the understanding of work and salvation?

4. Why did work have such spiritual significance for the Puritans? Why were the Puritans such active participants in the development of capitalism?

5. Why did the Protestant work-ethic become secularized? What led Tocqueville to prophesy that government would increasingly undertake the promotion of the work-ethic?

6. If a work-ethic cannot be validated, what is the role of work today?

7. Does the author convince you that contemporary economic realities do not sustain the notion of the primacy of work and the notion of deferred reward? Why or why not? Refer to page 53.

8. What is the peculiar role which American youth are playing in the transformation of the work-ethic? Why is this happening now? Would you agree there is a "youth consciousness" toward work, as the author and other observers suggest?

9. The author scrutinizes popular notions about leisure and finds them wanting. Why does he consider it false and mis-

leading to think of leisure as free time? Why is a production-consumption cycle, the logical conclusion of leisure, understood as having value in its relationship to work? What does leisure--understood as mere entertainment--say about our understanding of man? Is the author's examination adequate and helpful?

10. The author observes that many "never seem to experience any real leisure, but simply burn themselves out trying to work harder and play harder" (p. 67). Why are the symptoms of work addiction and other work "neuroses" so difficult to see in ourselves?

11. Discuss "Leisure is rather that sense of freedom which is realized when a person experiences more fully both his uniqueness and worth as an individual and his acceptance and relationship as part of the world around him" (p. 70). What context does this provide for work? Play? Worship?

12. Leisure, understood as a quality or style of life, reduces the distinction between work and play. In what ways does one's understanding of leisure determine the style of his working and playing?

13. Dahl believes that economic, social, and spiritual freedom focused in leisure is adequate for understanding the leisure revolution. Do you agree? Why or why not?

14. Is the concept of *leisure* as *freedom* viable for an increasingly secular society, since it is basically a spiritual concept? Why or why not?

Identify the main themes. Focus on aspects of the emerging leisure-ethic, and identify resources for a Christian life-style in a leisure-oriented society.

Questions for discussion or further thought:

1. Why have certain aspects of the emerging leisure-ethic been most visible in recent American counterculture?

2. The developing leisure-ethic which the author describes radically affirms personal freedom and dignity and promotes pluralistic value systems and diverse life-styles. What are the hazards of "doing your own thing"? The benefits? Would you limit this emphasis on individualism? Why or why not?

3. How does a leisure-oriented society promote the interdependence of men and groups? What relationship does the author see between the personal and corporate dimensions of the leisure-ethic?

4. The author believes that pluralism of values and life-styles will not result in anarchy. Do you agree or disagree? What opportunities does pluralism present?

5. What resources do Christians have for more honest, free, and perhaps less permanent relationships? Why does the leisure-ethic replace group loyalties with ecumenical and cosmopolitan attitudes?

6. Which aspects of the leisure-ethic do you find most difficult to affirm? Which are most difficult to ignore or deny? What is the challenge before us that is presented by freedom?

7. What do the Christian concepts of *abandon, beauty,* and *celebration* each contribute toward a new understanding of leisure?

8. What do you understand Dahl to mean when he says "Men cannot experience leisure until they learn to travel light" (p. 96)?

9. Why is *celebration* a difficult concept for many Christians?

10. The author insists that the concept of *Christian freedom* must become more radical than ever before. What are the elements of the life-style he desires? In what are their roots?

11. The author contends that a prophetic ministry toward "virtuous materialism" is imperative. What viable alternatives to the consumption-production cycle can you propose?

12. What kind of leisure ministry, or style of life, do you think the author would consider valid if he decries traditional ministries merchandized in leisure settings (pp. 104-105)?

13. What view of ministry does the author find most conducive to his understanding of mission in a leisure-oriented world? If clergy are viewed as facilitators, what is the role of laity? Why is voluntarism possibly the key to ministry in a leisure age?

14. If your group has met together for study and discussion in traditional patterns, would you consider a different format for your next (and final) session? Can you experience leisure and conclude your reflection on work and play? Could some members of your group create an appropriate worship experience? If there is interest, and if it would enrich your common life together, plan for this.

*Evaluate the main themes, focusing on work and play under-
stood as response to a gracious and caring God.*

Questions for discussion and further thought:

1. The author believes that "the crucial task for Christians
will be to establish appropriate relationships and priorities
among them in order to facilitate authentic experiences of
fulfillment and transcendence" (p. 112). How should work be
viewed to undertake this task? What is the role of play? Work?

2. What resources has the group appropriated from the study
to affirm work and leisure? Is it more possible to experience
work as play, to see play as worship, and to make worship our
work? Why? Identify insights the group has gained in understanding the leisure revolution.

3. Comment on the quotation from Professor Johnson: "It sometimes appears that Americans are enjoying the highest standard
of low living in history" (p. 114).

4. What new or revised forms of work, play, and worship do
group members want to see accomplished in the community? Is
anyone willing to undertake the educational and political
task necessary to work toward the desired change? Have personal life-styles been affected by this study?

5. Discuss how an appreciation of a leisure-oriented society
will enable the church "to raise its life and mission in this
world to new heights of ecstasy" (p. 116).

6. Ask yourselves if you have been "leisurely" in your reflection on *Work, Play, and Worship.*

7. The bibliography contains excellent resources for further
consideration of the leisure revolution. For another type of
group experience consult a film catalog. Many recent films,
such as "Sisyfos," "How Much Is Enough," "Questors," "The Cry
of the Marsh," "And Then They Forgot God," and "The Eighth
Day" provoke discussion on some of the issues raised in this
study. (The films listed are available from Augsburg Films.)

Code   10-7291